TAKING CARE *of* BUSINESS

Paul Cheetham-Karcz

NEW HAVEN PUBLISHING LTD

Published 2019
New Haven Publishing Ltd
www.newhavenpublishingltd.com
newhavenpublishing@gmail.com

Editor Martin Morrison
Cover design ©Neil McAdam

newhaven
publishing

ISBN: 978-1-912587-19-3

I'd like to dedicate this book to a number of people.

Firstly, to two very inspirational people who are no longer with us—my grandad and my nanna—who taught me everything I needed to know about old-school morals, and without whom I would only be half the person I am today.

To my mum and dad, who unselfishly gave their lives so I could have a better life.

To my wife, Zeri, who has not only been a rock to me but also helps shape my three amazing boys—Ethan, Rocco and Romeo—and they are the reason for everything that I do.

Paul Cheetham-Karcz

Contents

Introduction

Who the hell is Paul Cheetham-Karcz?

You won't recognise my name, you will not have heard of me, and you will have no idea of my business. And that's exactly why I feel this is the right time to write this book!

To be clear, I don't consider myself successful yet. In any case, what I deem as being successful has changed and evolved constantly throughout my career, and probably because of my working-class background, to even consider myself successful makes me cringe.

Yet, here I am, writing this book, advising you on how to build your business and how to live your life. So why am I writing this book? Well, there are a few reasons. I am new to the success game and the struggle still feels very real.

I have read a lot of autobiographies and have loved reading those written by the likes of Sir Richard Branson, Duncan Bannatyne OBE, and Peter Jones CBE—one that I would recommend, by the way, is *Shoe Dog* by Nike co-founder Phil Knight—but few of them actually scope out the hardship it takes to get to the top.

Quite often, I find these entrepreneurs are older by the time they write their memoirs, so perhaps time has chipped away at their memories of the struggles they faced earlier in their journeys as business owners. While the stories of people who are worth billions and have their own private islands are inspiring and entertaining, sometimes it all seems just a little too far away to be achievable.

I feel that now is the right time to write a book about the challenges facing entrepreneurs—because I'm still living and breathing it.

It's hard to see through the bullshit and #fakenews...

Social media has changed the game of the entrepreneur. Nowadays, the content on various social media platforms, including the likes of YouTube and LinkedIn, mostly presents a narrative of constant success and positivity. I think there is a fine line between self-promotion and marketing and telling the truth.

It seems to be fashionable for some to come up with an idea, raise some money from investors and private equity, rent a luxurious house, drive a prestige car, travel the world (sometimes business class or first class!) on this private equity money, and post all over their social profiles just how successful they are.

When you look further into these people's affairs you see that their companies, albeit sometimes showing potential, are posting huge losses and are in financial difficulty. Perhaps it's the accountant's part of my brain kicking in, but what I see in many of these cases is a financial reality that doesn't reflect the image that is being portrayed.

Please don't get me wrong—for those people who are genuinely successful, I love following their stories. Take, for example, the Kamani family who became successful with BooHoo.com and now operate billion-pound global businesses. I look at them with admiration, as well as with a slight touch of envy of course—because every post I see where they are posting a picture of themselves on Instagram with an A-list celebrity, I also see stock market reports where they are increasing profits, improving share prices, and dominating market share.

The Kamani family are the epitome of how it should be. Be successful, and then inspire. That's what I love. I happen to know of the family, be it very slightly, and I am also aware of the humble beginnings they started from and how hard they have had to work to get to where they are today. It's a truly inspiring story and one that is worthy of sharing. The fact is that they *are* successful (more on the definition of success later!), and their content actually just reiterates their reality, but that's not always the case.

...so I want to use this book to tell it how it is

On my social media platforms, if I have had a good month, I will post that I have had a good month, and if it's poor, I am not ashamed to say we had a poor month. If I am going to tell everyone when things are going well, why should I hide when things aren't going so well? For every post of me on my holidays in Monaco, why shouldn't I also tell people I am going out of my comfort zone and shitting myself because I have volunteered, for example, to give a public speech—something that I am really not comfortable with? Surely, it's in the best interest of the consumer to understand everything that is going on, right?

Perhaps, I am a throwback to the old way of doing things (the accountant in me rearing up again). But don't the large majority of us just have an idea, put our first purchases on our credit cards, work our arses off, feel as though we're getting nowhere, keep hitting brick walls, gain traction, create financial stability, risk it all again, get stressed out to fuck, hit some more brick walls, work doggedly to overcome them and build our companies from the foundation upwards—*we* still exist, don't we?

The life of the entrepreneur is littered with problems, stress, worry over bills, staff issues, funding issues, product issues—issues, issues, and more issues with the occasional light at the end of the tunnel spurring us on.

Shit! You still don't know who I am...

Then let me explain a little bit about me. I am from very working-class beginnings and I won't disrespect people who are working at all hours for £20k a year by pretending that I have not achieved a degree of success. To me, that would be disrespectful of my roots, so for the purpose of this book, I will accept that I am a success. In the real world, I actually find it easier to label myself "semi-successful".

Sedulo Group, the company I started in 2009, has EBITDA[1] of over £1 million per year. On that basis, I will accept that we, as a company, are doing better than most.

I am a non-executive director of a handful of other companies that have a combined turnover of around £50m. Many of these are achieving 100% year-on-year growth, and I am hoping some of them will become the corporate stars of the future.

I have a weekly podcast, not coincidentally called "Taking Care of Business", where I am fortunate enough to interview people connected to the world of Sedulo, who talk through their stories of inspiration. Some are business success stories, and others are purely inspirational people, but regardless of which category they fall within, there are common themes that run throughout both, which I will share with you.

As I sit here today, I have just turned 40 years old, I am newly married (with three amazing boys), and Sedulo is almost beginning to give me the financial freedom I've been craving. I say "almost" because as you will discover when you read this book, I don't think the fear of losing everything and having to start all over

---

1 EBITDA Earnings before Interest, Taxation, Depreciation, and Amortisation—the measure of a company's operating profitability.

again ever really leaves you. I have learnt to accept that it will probably always be this way, and as a result, I am not afraid of the anxiety this fear causes as much as I once was.

...or why you should read this book!

I am going to share with you some of the ups and downs I have experienced on my own journey. When I started writing this book, I thought *Fucking hell! This story is so erratic!* Then I realised that's how it should be because that is a true representation of the reality. This book is a roller coaster of chapters, and that's exactly how it has been. In fact, it's exactly as it still is!

There is this constant battle between becoming successful and looking after yourself—if you're reading this, then you probably want to do both. If you want my advice, you should absolutely do both—your health is your wealth.

This book deals with building businesses from the foundations upwards, painfully laying them down block by block, allowing you then to take calculated opportunistic risks along the way. In my opinion, this is the best way, despite some of the frustrations you might encounter on the journey, because the people I have seen make their wealth quickly have often lost it even faster.

If you're already on your journey, the chances are that you're already well aware of the mental strength and resilience that are required. If you are yet to start your business, be prepared for the emotional and personal battles you will have to deal with along the way. This book should give you some techniques to help you cope with them, or at very least, let you know that you're not alone in your struggle.

In order to become successful, you're going to need to make sure you take care of yourself, whilst taking care of business.

This book should help you with both.

Not so long ago, after telling one of my clients I was writing this book, they asked, 'What if I read your book and only find a couple of things I can take from it and don't like the rest?'

'That would be fantastic,' I replied. 'I don't expect anyone to take more than a few things from this book, and I doubt any reader is going to like it all.' As a result, I have included at the end of each chapter, what I consider, the most important actions you can take from that particular section.

This book describes a journey, so you just might come back to it at a later date and find two completely different aspects that are relevant and helpful in your life at that point. Now that would be amazing!'

Enjoy, and good luck on your journey!

Chapter I

About Sedulo

If you have come this far and you are still reading, I guess you will be wondering what I do.

It is inevitable, that I will disclose in the memoirs, events shared with particular clients and individuals, I do so with specific consent and authority to do so. As a professional advisor, confidentiality is paramount and I thank everyone within the book for allowing me to share their stories, in order that others gain a greater insight into the trials and tribulations of being an entrepreneur.

I run Sedulo, the firm that I set up in 2009. We are a team of advisors, operating from a main office in Manchester, another in Leeds, and a small satellite office in London. The team mainly comprises people who are qualified in accountancy, chartered tax, corporate finance, human resource, banking, and independent financial advice.

In 2017, Sedulo purchased Bartfields Accountants, a Leeds-based firm, which had a fee base of £2m and had been around for almost a century, and with that transaction our team grew to over 100 people.

Since setting up Sedulo, I have sold equity to the management team, so we now have a number of shareholders. Although I still own the majority of shares, I accept that as we grow my influence as a shareholder will naturally become more diluted, and I don't have any problem with that.

Our aim is simple. We help incubate businesses, and then we dealmake on their behalf. We either find the funding through private equity[2] or debt funders[3]—on average, we find funding for more than one UK business each working day—and offer our clients growth planning strategies throughout their journey.

When the time is right for the client, we sell the business, whole or part, and in some cases, we will guide our client towards a stock market listing. Around all this, we also act on the client's behalf, as individuals, and from a personal and family wealth-planning perspective.

We have around 2,000 clients, from start-ups to large companies, and we give advice globally. Sedulo acts on behalf of every kind of entrepreneur and business—from professional football league clubs, Super League rugby league clubs, and national governing bodies, to innovative and progressive technology and fashion

2 Private equity is composed of funds and investors that directly invest in private companies for equity stakes.

3 Debt funders are funders that borrow money to run your business but without taking equity stakes.

companies.

As for the individuals who we act for, our sport and media client base includes a wide range of people—from former England football managers, to fashion icons, recording artists, TV presenters, not to mention a whole host of Premier League footballers.

Our Manchester office is home to its own fully stocked New York-style bar, called "The Regency", a pool room, sweet shop, and our rooftop features another bar called "Randy's Reggae Shack". Our Leeds office has a "Great Gatsby Bar", "The Ambler Club", a chocolate shop, and an indoor Wimbledon-style table tennis court. The offices have won numerous accolades and underpin the "work hard-play hard" ethos that runs throughout the company.

How successful is Sedulo?

If I am going to write a book and suggest that some of the content being posted by other people who define themselves as successful is questionable, I think it's only fair that I share our financials with you!

The following chart shows Sedulo's turnover and profit level for every year from 2010 to the present, including the forecasted result for year end April 2019 and our projections for beyond...

Actual

	Revenue	Operating Profit
2010	£378,000	£110,000
2011	£484,000	£142,000
2012	£535,000	£185,000
2013	£723,000	£264,000
2014	£907,000	£335,000
2015	£1,044,000	£385,000
2016	£1,329,000	£407,000
2017	£2,019,000	£550,000
2018	£3,493,000	£821,000
2019	£7,000,000	£1,500,000

Forecast

2020	£9,900,000	£3,500,000
2021	£11,700,000	£3,900,000
2022	£14,100,000	£4,300,000

NB The profit figure shown for each year is the operating profit of the group prior to taxation and shareholder dividends.

Later in the book, I will go through the detail of how we grew areas of the business and built the company. For now, you can see from the table that it took us six years to break the £1m turnover milestone. It was incredibly hard work. and if I am honest, when I set out, I originally thought we would achieve this much quicker than we actually did.

I think it's a major milestone for a business like ours because once you get there, the business starts to feel like a "proper company" or at least it did to me. With circa 20 employees and almost 200 clients, word started to spread, and work started to come to us rather than me having to win each piece.

You can see the effect of this in the numbers because we then achieved £2m of revenue within two years of that original achievement.

Revenue growth was important to me because, as I will explain later, an accountancy firm is valued on its revenue and not its profit. This growth was, and still is, our main focus. Hence the revenue growth *every* year. Profit is important, though, and the business remained profitable throughout the period, although as more shareholders came on board, there was very little profit retained after dividends in the business.

For all those who are on the journey to get to that £1m milestone, the message throughout this book is to keep going! I can tell you, I worked harder for the years of 2010–2015, to get from £378k to £1m, than I did for the 2015–2019 years, when we took revenue from £1m to £7m.

The following illustration always comes to mind whenever I look back at our figures.

During the 2014/2015 period, I began to wonder whether running Sedulo was the best use of my time. It was growing at a painfully slow rate in comparison to the long hours I was working. I was being offered opportunities for financial director roles in technology companies that were progressing at a much more rapid rate than us, and I was wondering whether I was on the correct path to achieve what I wanted. I was nearly the guy above, and I did contemplate the alternative options that were available.

I am glad that I persevered, though, because once we broke through the pain barrier of £1m, we quickly gained traction as I have explained. What I didn't foresee, even at the time, was how quickly we would make that count.

I will share with you an extract of my diary from May 2016, when we had just completed our year end with a turnover of £1.3m.

If you excuse the scribble, you will see from my

notes that I had plotted out what each of our business areas would do through to 2021. These areas were tax, compliance accounting, corporate finance, management accounts, payroll/other and wealth management.

We set what we considered to be ambitious plans to grow to £1.91m in 2018, £2.3m in 2019, £2.6m in 2020, and to finally reach that figure of £3m in 2021. As you now know from our historical figures, we did £3.6m by 2018 and so we achieved our five-year plan within two years!

In 2019, we have put together a new three-year plan to 2022, which I have included in the figures. As opposed to the £3m we had originally wanted to achieve by 2021, we are now targeted to do £11.7m. We have a three-year plan to double revenue again from our current £7m revenue to £14.1m. It includes a mixture of incremental organic growth strategies and "level ups" in the form of a number of acquisitions we are planning. I will explain more about the requirement for "level ups" in your business later on in the book. You may also note that, due to the fixed cost base of our business, we expect to more than double our profits—something that has become gradually more important as we have grown in size.

Chapter II

About Me

As I mentioned earlier, it is highly likely that you haven't a clue who I am, so let me fill you in.

I was born 28th June 1978, in Stockport, Greater Manchester, in a working-class borough called Reddish. My mum, Elaine, was in her early twenties at the time, when she was still married to my biological father, also called Paul—Paul Karcz. I also have a sister, Michelle, who is six years older than me.

The relationship between my mum and Paul wasn't destined to last long, and by the time I had reached the age of two, my mum was bringing up two kids as a single parent.

The memories I have as a child are of my mum constantly battling to keep our heads above water by working as many hours as she could at the local off-licence, while being stuck in what seemed like a never-ending fight to get some child support from Paul senior. As I understand it, each time the authority that is now called the Child Maintenance Service (CMS) in the UK would chase him for money towards our upkeep, he would simply leave his job.

In the end, my mum was awarded 1p a year for both kids. Can you believe that—that a man could walk out of court, happy in the knowledge that he only had to pay 1p per year towards his kids? Now, as a dad myself, I can't think of anything worse. My original "Why?" was to provide as much as was physically possible for my wife and kids, as I will discuss in more detail later on.

I owe a lot to my mum...

What we lacked in money, however, my mum made up for in the love she gave us. She could not possibly have loved her kids any more than she did, just as she couldn't love her grandchildren any more than she does now, and I owe so much of what I have managed to achieve throughout my lifetime to her strength. She works within Sedulo, and now in her sixties, Mum has as much drive, if not more, than anyone in the business.

In the early days of the business, it was my mum who stopped me spending what we didn't have. I couldn't recommend anything more highly than to employ your mum. Mine is the gatekeeper of our business, and it feels special to know that we are working together on creating a legacy for our future generations.

For the record, I have no real negative thoughts towards Paul, and I have no positive ones either. It just is what it is. He had his reasons to do what he did, and

I have seen him maybe once (at my nanna's funeral) in the past 35 years. My feelings towards him are purely neutral. In fact, I feel no differently about Paul than I would about any random man walking past me in the street. I will, however, never understand why a man doesn't want to care for his children.

What I have realised lately, is that regardless of what I think of Paul in an adult headspace, the rejection I experienced as a young child has an effect on my behaviour today. I believe this lack of being accepted by him is what gives me the drive today to achieve and feel accepted. For sure, even today I am still not very good at handling rejection, and I carry insecurities that I can only attribute to my childhood experience. I have learnt to accept that this negative situation, which happened in my childhood, gave me the fire and determination that makes me the person I am today.

As a child, I lived with my mum and my sister in a two-bedroom house. I can still remember the second-hand, brown and orange sofa we used to have and the record player on the floor in the kitchen where we used to play the John Lennon record "Woman". I think we only had the one vinyl record, and it was constantly on repeat.

Sundays were when most of the cooking in our house was done, by Mum—enough to last the whole week. The finished article was a huge bowl of potato hash that we would warm up and begrudgingly eat every night thereafter. At the same time mum was preparing "tea" for the week ahead, we would get our weekly treat, which consisted of corned beef on toast. I can still remember how good it used to taste, and how bad the experience was of eating hash every other night of the week. Needless to say, it's no longer a part of my diet.

My mum saved up and got us a brown Austin Allegro car to get around in, which was a huge thing for us at the time, and I remember how chuffed we all were that we had a car—until one of us opened the door at the wrong time and a passing lorry took it off its hinges! For the rest of that car's lifetime, it had bright blue rope attaching the door to its frame, to stop it from falling off.

As my mum worked so much, I recall spending a lot of time with her dad, Grandad Bill. My grandad died when I was 13, but there isn't a day that goes by when I don't think of him. Like a lot of people his age in the late 70s and early 80s, he lived on a council estate. As a young man, Grandad had fought in the Second World War, and although he was only small, he was scared of no one. Just thinking about that reminds me of the time when a supposed local drug dealer moved into the house next door to Grandad.

Overall, everyone got on with each other on the estate, but there was this one time when things got a bit heated between this guy next door and my grandad, who was well into his sixties by then. The dealer said something about giving my grandad a good hiding, and Bill offered to take him up on that challenge there and then—nothing happened, but I love that about the older generation. They are real tough folk—made of solid moral fibre. A bit of mouth from a young upstart is nothing to them after what they have been through.

I believe the relationship I had with my grandad taught me to respect my elders. It certainly helped strengthen my moral fabric, and that it is something I take great pride in. It also encouraged me to gravitate towards experienced people, and today I find myself getting drawn in by people with more years on the clock than me to see what I can learn from them.

I spent a fair amount of time with my nanna too—Paul's mum—who lived close to my grandad. She seemed to compensate for the lack of financial support from Paul and would always give me money for treats. When I went to college and university, and I was one of the very few in my family who did, she paid my petrol money throughout. I owe a lot to my nanna and her husband Derek, who I affectionately called "Uncle Derek". Nanna was a fun but very headstrong character, and I guess some of this rubbed off on me.

She had flown over to New York to work in the diamond trade in the 1950s, a time when most people wouldn't know what an aeroplane was! It is another regret of mine that she passed away just as I was starting out in business, as she never got to see what her influence helped shape.

... and my "real" dad...

By the age of four, my life had picked up. There was a guy who lived on our street called Jack Cheetham, and I don't know why, but I used to run up to the top of the road, knock on his front door and say that my mum wanted to speak to him. It worked because in the end, they got together, have now been married for over 30 years, and he has been the greatest dad anyone could wish for. I have never met a more selfless man—another proper old-school bloke—and he would do anything for his stepchildren from the get-go. He is simply my dad, a real dad, and I can't pay him any greater compliment than that.

Once my mum and dad had got together, the financial hardship gradually eased off. Jack was a lorry driver, and Mum got herself a job in B&Q and worked her way up, so the holidays, cars and Christmases slowly got better.

Whilst I do have vivid memories about the not so good early years, I have no complaints about life after my mum met my dad. I had a good upbringing and my mum and dad gave me everything they possibly could.

I went to the local high school, Reddish Vale, and if I am honest, I only did what I needed to do to get the qualifications for the next stage. I played for the sports teams, hung out with the main gang and wasn't a teacher's pet by a long stretch. I was always aware that I wanted to be with the cool kids and didn't go out of my way to get fantastic GCSEs. Nevertheless, I comfortably got enough *A*'s and *B*'s to get me into college. *Job Done.*

... and the best work experience I could have ever had

I went back to the school awards dinner not long ago as a guest speaker—I try to give what I can back to the school, and they had asked me to give a speech—and I spoke on how not to fall into the system. I will mention throughout this book about how society seems to frown upon failure thus encouraging people to lower their own level of expectation. It's a system I don't partake in.

When I was a student at Reddish Vale, there seemed to be a focus on getting a job, and that was judged to be the measure of success. During what we called "fourth year"—what is now "year 10"—they sent me for work experience at a car mechanics garage in the hope that I might impress and get offered a job when I left school.

I sat there for two weeks, watching grown men count down the hours until home time, wishing their lives away. I watched them moan about how cold it was, how crappy their pay was, and how mistreated they felt. The negativity was all-encompassing, and I remember thinking to myself *there's no fucking way I am going to live my life like that!*

A-levels seemed to be the better option so that's what I chose to do next, but I didn't like college life much either. The people were not like me, in the main, and my mates all had jobs and were earning their own money. I would hardly go in—until exams that is. Then, when it mattered, I would do 16-hour days, reading books about the lectures I had missed. I ended up with two *A*'s and a *C*, which gave me an overall score of 26 points out of a possible 30, when I only needed 20, I think, to get into university—*another job done!*

At the time, I wanted to be involved in sport in some way. My interest in sport guided me to do a sport science degree at university with the hope of becoming a PE teacher. I have got to be honest—at university, it felt as though I fitted in even less. Most people there appeared to be well off and from wealthier upbringings than the one I'd had. They also messed about a lot, and that wasn't really for me—I was there to get the qualification and move on, not to make new friends. Many of them seemed much more immature than I felt I was at the time, so I hardly went in. When I did go in, I'd copy the notes of some of the few friends I had there, and Matt Wilson, whose brother Dan is now a partner at Sedulo, should have probably graduated with two degrees in the end—his own and another for helping me out! Still, I got my degree and to me that was just another box ticked. It was time to enter the real world!

Chapter III

Find a Winning Formula

When you are getting started, I think it is very important to develop a structure of what works best for you. If you look at many of today's business-related television programmes, you will notice that the key personalities of these shows tend to replicate a winning formula.

Take Gordon Ramsay's *Kitchen Nightmares*, for example. As entertaining as it is, every show follows the same methodology. He finds a struggling restaurant and adopts the same techniques every time to bring about positive change, regardless of the situation. Ramsay has developed and refined a winning formula, and he uses this as his template for success on all future projects.

Each time I chat with someone on my weekly podcast, regardless of the difference in their actual activity, the same things come up time and time again.

I also discovered a set of basic business principles

in my first role, and just as Ramsay has, I have applied these to most of the business situations I have encountered ever since.

Just to be clear, I am not about to share anything ground-breaking with you. I use very simple, and obvious, techniques. There are very few special people in the world, and I am not one of them. Over the course of my life, I have learnt that the majority of people who become successful are not the ones who have inherited a God-given talent, but the ones who learn to do the simple things well.

To set the scene, I had left university with a sports science degree, and I didn't know where to turn. I saw an advert for a graduate job—to train to become an accountant. If I'm honest, I didn't even know what an accountant was. Nevertheless, I applied, and I somehow got the job. Now I was to become a trainee accountant in the debt management industry.

The whole industry was built around one particular piece of legislation that made it impossible for a creditor to refuse if borrowers who were struggling to meet their repayment obligations offered to pay a lower amount than they could afford in order to reduce their indebtedness.

To take the stress away, a debt management company would then tell the client to pass over all their debt collection correspondence, and the company would then sort it and remove the emotional burden that being in debt causes.

Simple right? With the exception that back in the late 90s, it seemed as though everyone was in debt above their eyeballs, and they couldn't repay it. The emergence of the debt management industry would help everyone sleep at night, happy in the knowledge that they could now pay off their debt over 40 years. It was a consumer's dream, and the industry could barely keep up with the demand. We got about 50,000 client sign-ups in no time.

My first role was within the internal audit department of the company. Because the industry was frowned upon by the lenders, and lacked regulation as it was brand new, the company wanted to get the ISO 9002 award to prove its credibility. The directors set up an internal audit department to get it, and about ten of us were tasked with the process.

Don't be afraid to drive through change

After successfully completing a project in internal audit, the department head came to see me. He said he was impressed with my work ethic and asked if I could run a six-month project. I accepted, of course, and then they told me I was to be the manager of the post room. At the time, I didn't care *what* I was managing. I was wearing a suit for work, and I was now being called a manager!

As I have already explained, the company had gained 50,000 sign-ups rapidly, and each client, on average, had seven different creditors. As a minimum, there would be seven pieces of correspondence per client per month because they all received a statement from each creditor every month. It was most likely, however, that they would be chased throughout the month and issued with all sorts of legal threats and default notices so the figure was much higher. We didn't deal too much in emails in those days, so everything was organised by post.

As I was excitedly walking down to the post room to find out about my new position, my line manager at the time informed me that there was a problem with, as he gleefully described them, "the numpties in the business".

The post room was the first point of contact for the clients, but it was also where the business employed the ones who everyone referred to as "the numpties"! Unfortunately, they were six weeks behind in opening the mail and correctly distributing it to the twenty or so departments within the business where it could then be processed. By the time that mail had reached the relevant department, it was fair to say that the follow up piece of correspondence had already been sent out to the client concerned, and neither had yet been opened nor dealt with. It was a *huge* problem.

When I walked into the room, I could see the extent of the issue. There were hundreds of thousands—and I *mean* hundreds of thousands—of envelopes, bills and statements littered everywhere. Twenty people just sat there staring at me. Some of the younger lads looked like tough guys, almost as though they would rather break out into a scrap than cooperate with anything I had to say. They hated their job and some, I think, hated their lives. That's how it looked to me.

For the first few days, I just looked at the enormity of the thousands of letters a day coming in—maybe half of them getting dealt with, and the other half just adding to the pile of unopened and unprocessed mail. I looked at the "I don't give a fuck" approach and attitude of every single member of the team, and my heart sank with every hour I spent with them. They'd come in late, if they bothered to turn up, and half the time they looked as though they had come in straight from a night out.

After a week of observing, I thought *fucking hell*—nothing had changed, the pile of mail had just got bigger, the staff were still as disengaged as ever, and I started to feel that the task was too big. I didn't have any answers, and I was starting to panic.

That was when I decided, right there and then, that I was going to do something. I wasn't certain what, but I wasn't about to sit on my hands and watch everything fall to pieces around me. *Something* had to change.

I didn't have a clue what I was doing. I just decided to make some changes, and success followed instantly. These small changes became the basic business principles that I have applied to almost every role or situation I have found myself in ever since.

Instil discipline and self-respect

The first thing I knew I had to do was to establish some rules. We had to rebuild an identity. The current one was not good, and it was self-perpetuating. The staff within the post room team stood out a mile from the rest of the company who were all in suits—this lot were in tracksuit bottoms and sports trainers. It was the uniform of numpties. They looked like numpties, were labelled as numpties, and they acted up to the label.

Now, a lot has changed over the years, and people

dress differently in workplaces these days. I am a big fan of the dress-down code, but when you're bringing discipline into a business, you have to start with a tight grip until obedience flows through the spine of the firm. Then you can relax it carefully, and that's what I did.

I implemented a strict dress code, and if anyone didn't adhere to it, they would be sent home unpaid. Lateness was constant, and sick days were high, so I told them that any lateness or unauthorised sickness would be dealt with through disciplinary action. At the same time, I made sure I was first in, last out, and the best-dressed in the department. I lead the way by behaving in the way I expected them to behave. I believe in leading by example.

Things are not that strict at Sedulo because everyone already knows what is expected—discipline is a part of our culture and runs through our veins, so we can take a more relaxed and adult approach to the dress code and flexible working. But in the case of the post room, that kind of trust would have been abused.

When the former Manchester United manager, Sir Alex Ferguson, arrived at the club, he inherited some great players. But the story goes that he also inherited a team with a drink culture—he cut that out immediately.

The first thing Ferguson did was to get rid of anyone who didn't adhere to the culture he was about to create. He was also known for having a fiery temper, but that was mainly in the earlier days. Once he established the authority and discipline, he was able to relax his grip—subsequent players describe him as being more of a father figure—and yet the discipline was maintained. I am a big fan of his methodology, and I adopted this within the post room.

Make people accountable

The second thing I did was to announce a change in *everyone's* job role. All post room work had previously been divided in such a way that one person, for example, would just open envelopes for 7.5 hours a day, another would only be date-stamping correspondence for 7.5 hours a day, while another more experienced person would be responsible for sorting all the correspondence out, so it could be sent to the relevant departments—hopefully!

I couldn't work out from this system whose output was good and whose wasn't—it was an immeasurable task. It was also bloody boring for everyone, having to face the same tedious task, hour after hour, day after day!

I told everyone that, with immediate effect, they were responsible for opening, stamping, sorting and delivering their own mail. This new approach helped reduce the tedious nature of the work, but more importantly it allowed me to measure their work by the number of bundles they got through, and all of a sudden each of them could see whether they were in front or behind their co-workers, and output as a whole increased dramatically.

When you introduce measurables, you will be surprised what effect that has on productivity of a team. It is surprising how many companies don't have good measurement structures in place for performance.

The staff within the post room also had to personally deliver the mail, so when they dropped the mail off at the wrong department, they were the ones who had to face the head of that department. They quickly learned that it was easier for them just to get it right in the first place—because they became accountable for their own actions.

Now, you might be sat there wondering, *does he think we are fucking stupid? This is advice for dummies!* And yet, if you look around your business today, it's likely there are some members of your team who have the ability to hide behind someone else, and you can bet your bottom dollar that productivity will be less because of it.

Recognise and reward people

By making people accountable, I could now also successfully monitor their performance. The next step was to introduce some simple reporting methods.

I displayed both the team and the individual performance on a screen, so everyone could see who had done what during the day. We logged when each bundle was sorted and distributed, and by whom.

Team members were split into three divisions, and we produced a league table to show performance. Each week, someone was selected for relegation or promotion across the divisions, based on the number of bundles produced by individuals.

The winner of "Division 1" got £30 worth of vouchers, for coming top in "Division 2" they got £20, and the "Division 3" winner got either a bottle of wine or a crate of beer according to their preference.

I paid for the prizes out of my own pocket—I

was on £12,000 per year at the time. Some of the supervisors, who were probably no older than 20 years old, began to chip in. We were creating a team.

I don't suppose many people were truly hell-bent on getting £30 worth of vouchers or a crate of beer, yet the initiative worked, and everyone upped their game. It was the principle of competition that created the uplift in performance.

Often, people think it is the size of the prize that motivates staff, and I am sure that in some instances it does—but, in my experience, that is not always the case, and it is predominantly the recognition that is the motivating factor.

We introduced our own service level agreements with other departments, and a customer satisfaction report went out each day to the other departmental managers. The post room was to become its own business unit within a business, with a focus on providing quality customer service to the rest of the company.

Again, these are all very basic principles, but how many companies carry out staff satisfaction surveys or client satisfaction surveys, and out of those that do, how many constantly communicate performance feedback to their staff? Do you? If you don't, you should. They are amazing for monitoring performance and for recognising excellence or development requirements within teams.

Since then, across a plethora of businesses, I have organised reward packages based on sales targets, billing targets, and profit shares—and I have put in place share options schemes for my clients. These are all equally valid tools, and they are all built on the basic principle of measuring, reporting, and rewarding performance.

Educate and develop people

There's an old story I once heard, about a conversation between the CFO and COO of a business. It runs along the following lines:

> **CFO asks CEO: "What happens if we invest in developing our people and then they leave us?"**
>
> **CEO: "What happens if we don't, and they stay?"**

I don't think any half-decent CFO has ever asked such a question, but the story still puts a valid message across. Yet, in many businesses, personal development plans for employees either don't exist or they are a box-ticking exercise.

Personal development plans are part of the very essence of Sedulo and are put in place by our HR function. But I don't mean those task-driven exercises that make you feel as though you're doing something right even if you're not, either. What I mean is personal training plans that are relevant and include content that is exciting to the staff—designed to promote genuine development.

If I am given training development plans to

quickly look over, and I *do* because they are crucial to our progress, and there are things included that I wouldn't be excited about doing, we redo them. It's a simple as that.

In order to get what I wanted from those that worked in the post room, I had to give more than I expected to receive. I had to make sure they were getting the development they desired and required.

Establish a give and take relationship

As an employer, I advise you to give first and take later.

It seemed like common sense to me that there would have to be some give and take in the new relationship that was forming between the soon-to-be-former post room numpties and their new management.

I figured that if they now had to come in on time, dress smart, get measured on performance, increase their output, and improve their general behaviour, we needed to offer them something more than a few crates of beer and a gift voucher. Because employing a team is all about balance, and if my team are giving more to me than they are receiving from me over a prolonged period of time, they are going to be pissed off. And I would feel the same if that situation was reversed.

Without balance, you end up with an environment where the bosses are fed up with the staff and the whole team is fed up with the bosses—and that takes me all the way back to year 10 again at that mechanics garage, and that was not for me.

So I registered them all for an NVQ business administration course in a local college. Every single one of them was registered on the course. You know what? They won award after award, and every one of them gained the qualification in record time within the college. They stayed in the office until late at night after work and helped each other with their homework—it created a team bond. It gave them self-respect. It created willing staff.

We didn't have any IT equipment in the office, and the staff were not computer literate, and yet these people, in the main, were young adults in their late teens and early twenties. I went to the IT department and found three old, discarded desktop computers that still worked, and then I put a system in place where all the staff would get training on them twice a week.

Reap the rewards

A major transformation followed almost instantaneously. The team started to arrive on time, smartly dressed. They would open, stamp, and sort the mail before delivering it personally to each of the departmental heads, along with a document to review the quality of their work. They would talk about who was doing the most, who had finished their homework first, and who could do what on a computer—they came together.

Remarkably, within a week, we actually got to the point where the mail that came in on a given day went out to the relevant departments on that same day. We were then able to start tackling the backlog of mail, which had accumulated over time.

Within another week, we had got all that week's mail out and caught up with one week of the backlog.

Within six weeks, we had reached a point where all the mail that had ever come into the business had been opened, stamped, sorted, checked, and delivered to the correct department.

We could finally see the walls and floor of the office, so we painted it together to make it look even smarter. We brought in a radio, and twice a day, we would play games like "Name That Song" to have a bit of fun. The post room became a nice place to work. The young, aggressive kids from the likes of Salford and Newton Heath, real working-class Manchester suburbs, began to smile and enjoy their work, and get the job done. More importantly, they began to develop as staff and as people.

It got even better because over the next few months I managed to secure a pay rise for quite a few of them. The improved performance of the department hadn't gone unnoticed across the wider business, and other managers were starting to recognise and compliment members of our team. This resulted in two members leaving the department to join the finance function, another going into the human resource department, and one other going to the IT division—this had been completely unthinkable just a few months earlier.

The "numpties" were no more.

Establish your winning formula

I still remember how good it felt to see what we had managed to achieve, and I still consider what I did with the post room as my greatest achievement, regardless of the fact that later on I went on to do things worth much more financially and on a much grander scale.

I learnt the basic principles of business and leadership that worked for me, and despite having worked on more glamorous and financially rewarding projects since, I have never forgotten them, and I revisit them often. I had learnt my winning formula.

Take action...

1. Drive through change

After a week or so in my role as post room manager, I had changed nothing, and subsequent results obviously hadn't changed either. It was only when I had the courage to make decisions and push them through, to give my ideas a go, that a positive difference was made. You have got to be true to yourself, and do what you feel is right in the situation.

2. Educate and develop people

Everybody wants to be paid well, so if you don't pay people what they deserve, you run the risk of them being unhappy and producing reduced performance. However, even highly paid employees become disillusioned when they don't see their own personal progression. In my experience, formal, agreed training and development is perhaps even more important to a motivated workforce than the simple matter of pay.

Chapter IV

Get Started

You have got to start somewhere.

There are many different reasons for starting your own business and you will have your own, so am not going to give you a list of reasons of why you should. However, I am going to start with an example of why I believe you shouldn't.

Why you shouldn't get started

We have an events space in our Manchester office called The Regency Club. It is a New York-style bar area, which we use as an events and workspace for our clients, staff and business partners to either drop in and work from or to hold meetings.

At one of our events, I was running a Q&A session, and a smart-looking young lady in the audience asked me if we could meet at some point in the future to discuss a project of hers.

We went for coffee, and she explained that she was an accountant for PWC, one of the "Big Four" accounting firms, and she was wanting to leave them to start her own business.

'That's great,' I said. 'Doing what?'

'I'm not sure,' she replied. 'I just want a business that's mine.'

Digging deeper, I asked her, 'Why?'

'Well you can work when you want and get paid more money,' she announced, enthusiastically.

I nearly spat my coffee out over the table. Here was an intelligent lady thinking that she was just going to start a business in something, anything, and earn more money than she could working at a company like PWC *and* work less hours!

Where do people get these misconceptions from? Perhaps it's the social media effect—update after update of business leaders putting all this one-sided, positive content out there, usually synonymous with celebrity lifestyles, from within businesses that are yet to achieve the kind of success they portray. As mentioned earlier in the introduction to this book, I think the image projected is far from the truth. It certainly seems to be, from what I see day in, day out, in the offices of Sedulo and across our client base.

There are plenty of examples within our customer base of really hard-working clients—clients who work 80 hours a week in the office, employing 50–100 staff, that rely on them, and who have personal guarantees on their family home should it all go wrong. Some of these people earn between £30k and £40k per year, and they can only pay themselves this when the cash is available. It goes without saying in business, that as the owner of the business, you get paid last—if at all.

It was a rare occasion, during the first two to three years of running my own business, that I got paid on time.

So I am going to put it out there, now—if your motivation to set up a business is to instantly lead a better life by getting paid more for doing less, forget it!

Don't let fear hold you back

One of my favourite quotes, which is displayed on the wall of The Jordan Suite in our Manchester office, puts it well:

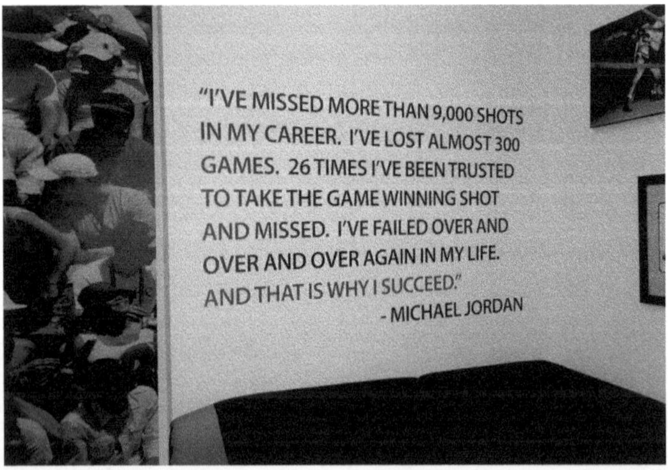

It constantly amazes me how often the fear of failure holds people back from attempting to achieve their dreams. Perhaps it's the system, indoctrinating us from a young age to lower our ambitions, as I mentioned earlier. Perhaps it's the social media effect again that seems to encourage us to wallow in other people's dismay.

Before I had the same understanding of fear as I have today, I used to see it as a negative emotion. As I have interviewed more people on my podcast, I have come to realise that fear is normal, and I feel as though I have developed a healthy relationship with the fear of failure.

I now see fear of failing as a positive, something that stays by my side and constantly gnaws at me enough to abandon any thoughts of complacency. If you learn to embrace fear and use it to your advantage, it can become a healthy tool for success.

We all have a fear, but some of us have more courage than others to continue despite it, and this resilience is a major contributing factor to who succeeds and who doesn't.

A reason to get started

Setting up my business came naturally to me, despite me not knowing of anyone else, at that time, who had ever done it. I had spent three years working within an industry role within the debt management business before qualifying to be an accountant, and then choosing to work for a further three years in an accountancy practice. The difference between the two was massive. They were like chalk and cheese.

When you take on a finance role within a business, it tends to be very hands-on, and the figures you produce will be used to make key decisions. I didn't get a buzz from doing the numbers bit. That came later when the numbers were fed through, and we could start making decisions on what to do next or we could track in detail the effect of a decision we had made before. I loved being a part of making a difference to other people's journey, and that's something I will come back to later in the book.

Anyway, coming back to working in practice, my work wasn't having any effect on my clients, so after three years I decided it was time to find an accountancy firm that was genuinely focused on changing its clients' lives.

I am sure this will be controversial, but I honestly couldn't find one. Perhaps they do exist and I just happened to miss them in my search, but I can only be honest and say I looked all over and I couldn't find one. The huge accountancy firms cover all advisory areas for those who can afford it, but I wanted to work with clients that were on their way up—not having already made it.

The conclusion I came to was that there wasn't an offering in the industry that provided forward thinking, or hands-on entrepreneurial advice, to the growing businesses, delivered in a personable manner.

Listen to your gut instinct

So, just like that, I thought *Fuck it! I'm gonna do it! If it doesn't exist, I am going to bring it to the table. I'm gonna start my own business!*

Making that decision came very naturally to

me, but I can't remember one defining moment where I made the call because I don't think there was one.

One day, I just decided to hand my notice in at work and take a chance. I had no idea whether I would be any good at running my own company, and I didn't dwell too much on that because if I had, I may well have decided against it.

And so, that was what prompted me to start Sedulo. Whether you are setting a business up to improve your wealth, create a legacy, fill a gap in the market, or change the world, I advise you to listen to your gut instinct first. There are many times throughout this book when I will make reference to this, because it has rarely failed me.

Take advantage of opportunity

In 2018, I was fortunate enough to host an Empowered Women event for Leeds Business Week, where I interviewed female entrepreneur Sophie Whittam who is the founder of a company called Fight Label.

Sophie had been a figure skater in her early years, and having struggled to find outfits, she began to make them for herself. It wasn't long before she was making outfits for the rest of her teammates who were representing Great Britain.

One evening, she was invited to a promotional event featuring world champion boxer Amir Khan. After chatting to her management team, they asked if she could make boxing shorts. Silly question as she had never made a pair of boxing shorts in her life—so she answered 'yes', of course!

She went on to make the world's most expensive boxing shorts, made out of 24-carat gold, for Khan's bout in Las Vegas against another former world champion, the US boxer Devon Alexander.

Watching, that night, was arguably one of the greatest fighters of all time, Floyd Mayweather, who promptly instructed his management team to appoint Fight Label to make the shorts for his next fight.

Sophie now has a full team in Sheffield, and they make gear for the top 1% of boxing's elite, including the likes of heavyweight superstars Anthony Joshua and Deontay Wilder, and they even made the sportswear for the fight scenes in the Sylvester Stallone-produced blockbuster Creed II—needless to say, she no longer finds time to make figure skating outfits.

It's a great story that shows how being in the right place at the right time, and then leveraging that fortune to your advantage, can bring real success. We display a quote from Sir Richard Branson that relates to this, on the wall of The Branson Suite at our Manchester office:

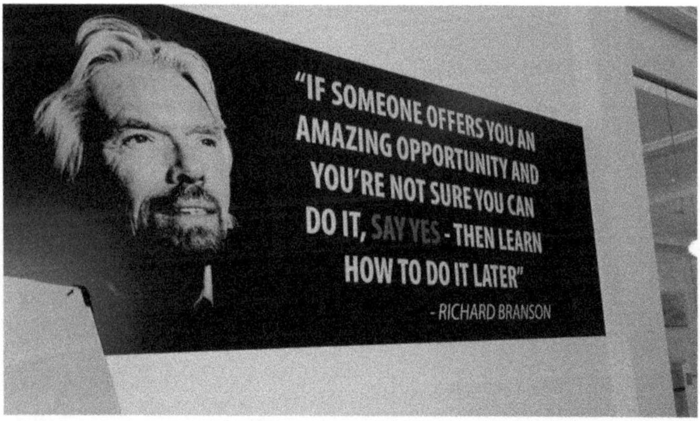

In my opinion, this is how the biggest successes are made, not the manufactured start-ups.

Believe in yourself

During the first 8–12 weeks at Sedulo, I worked from home and I hated it. My brain couldn't decide whether I was supposed to be working or relaxing, and I felt very mixed up and a little off-centre during this short period. I quickly realised that when I walk through the front door of my home, I need to feel that I am entering a place of relaxation. Although I still work from home every evening, for the first few steps after I've walked through that front door, I feel as though a valve within me is releasing some of the pressure, ever so slightly. Working from home wasn't for me.

In my head, Sedulo was always going to be big, and something beyond a business that relied upon me. I have no idea why the notion came to me, but again, it was more of an instinctive gut feeling that came from within. I was so optimistic back then when I started that we took a pretty big risk and rented an office on Deansgate in the centre of Manchester with enough room for at least 20 staff. That was quite a brave decision, looking back, more so because we signed a 5-year lease without a break clause on a new start-up business and I personally guaranteed it—along with a bank overdraft.

Again, I have spoken to many business owners, and those who believe in themselves and take the risks seem to be those who do the best in the end. When I signed the lease for the new office, I didn't have a care in the world for the documents or the risks I was signing.

I would have signed anything put in front of me. I was unwavering in my belief that it would work—I didn't have a fallback position so it just *had* to work.

This is one of the reasons why I believe owning a business should be less of a conscious and rational decision, and more like something that is just done instinctively. If it's a conscious decision, you are more likely to fully grasp the reality of the situation. If I had analysed things sensibly, I would have either never gone ahead and done it or I would have done it on a smaller scale.

I went out and got myself a personal credit card for £10,000. We managed to get hold of some cheap laptops and second-hand furniture, and we painted all the walls and varnished the rotten, chipped desks. Our boardroom table cost £50 and had a chunk missing out of it. It looked like a surfboard that had been bitten by a shark! So we bought some red fabric and draped it over the table, and—job done—we had a boardroom! For some reason, we painted the skirting boards and other woodwork gold.

Dare to be different

The boardroom had red fabric everywhere (covering the cracks and holes in our furniture), gold woodwork and varnished desks—not your typical accountants—and it definitely made an impression, albeit looking more like a brothel than an accountant's office!

Around that time, I came across a sports law firm called Brabners. After a little more research on Google, I discovered that one of the partners there, Maurice

Watkins, was also on the board of Manchester United Football Club, and I decided to give them a call.

I told them we were a new player in the market and that they needed to meet with us because we were going to be something special in Manchester. They agreed to see us, and one of the founding partners, Robert Street, came to meet us in our offices—it still makes me laugh to this day because of the look on his face as he walked in and looked around at the decor! Still, it worked because he brought another young lawyer with him (another partner at Brabners at the time), who turned out to be one of the best lawyers I know. That other lawyer is called Sam Mabon, and we have worked together ever since.

I wish I still had pictures that I could share to show how crazy, or ridiculous, our office looked. But I am very proud of what we did and the fact that we built the business from scratch with our own money and a shoestring budget. Not that I have a problem with attracting investment—we get investment for people all the time and it's something I am considering in the future for further acquisitions.

Both debt and private equity funding have a crucial part to play in the growth of businesses. It's just that I feel that some people become fixated on this idea that they can't get their business off the ground without investment. In my experience, there is usually a way around everything if you want it badly enough.

Once we had our own office and were all ready to go, I signed an agreement with my previous employer that allowed me to take one client with me as long as I left all the others. So Sedulo had its first client, a telecoms company, based in Cheshire, called Gteq Solutions, and they are still a client of ours to this day.

Our second client was a one-man-band graphic designer, and he is still a client, too—regardless of how much our firm has grown in size, we have never put his fees up and he still pays us his £50 a month on a standing order!

I enjoyed the whole start up piece, the hustle of signing new clients, choosing a business name, stepping out into the unknown. They were truly memorable days.

There was only one problem...I had chosen the wrong business partner!

Take action...

1. Don't let fear hold you back

Overthinking the situation can lead to paralysis. You must have the conviction to action your ideas and visions.

Failing doesn't mean you have failed. It often just means you have moved a step closer to success.

2. Dare to be different

In order to sell your product or service, it is highly likely you are going to need to have a unique selling point.

Have the courage to be a leader, an innovator, to be different—don't follow the crowd.

Chapter V

If it Doesn't Work, Start Again

Originally, I intended to set up Sedulo on my own. Then my manager, where I worked at the time, explained that he was up for us doing something together. We had a chat and that was that—we set up in partnership. It seemed like a safer option than doing it on my own. To add a third spoke to the wheel, we took on our first employee, Lee Jones, another colleague from the company we were working for at the time, and Sedulo version 1.0 was formed.

As I mentioned in the last chapter, there are lots of things to get excited about in the first year. There was this powerful sense of freedom and excitement, of just getting stuff done. We chose our name (deciding on a brand name rather than the typical Cheetham & Co.), the offices were opened, the website was launched, and we started signing up our first clients.

I remember walking around our offices, which were about 1500 square foot of floor space, painting them at the weekend, and experiencing this sense of wonderment that they were our offices. Even now, I can still recall the touch, feel and sensation of handling our first business cards—embossed with the letter *S* to make them feel expensive.

We had chosen our colour to be deep red, or crimson, because we had learned that it stood for royalty, nobility and warmth. Our name, Sedulo, was chosen because of its link to the Latin word "Sedulous", which means showing dedication and diligence. That seemed to fit with our shared ethos at the time.

When we launched Sedulo, my business partner and I had known each other and worked together for four or five years. We had a mutual respect for one another, and we often socialised together after work. It seemed like the perfect fit.

To be fair to him, he had lent me £10,000 to put down as a deposit on my first house, and so I owe him a lot from that perspective, and even today, I remain grateful for that act of trust and generosity. However, it didn't work out, and I am sure he will have his own opinion on why it didn't just as I have mine.

Agree on objectives

For a start, he was used to being my boss, and if I am honest, I think he thought he would still be in charge moving forward. He also started with a big client, and therefore the fees he had were far higher than mine. I remember my heart sinking as early as our first month when he was paying our wages out, and I had worked non-stop on doing background things such as the website, registering us with the Chamber of Commerce and banks, and sorting out the offices—he asked me how much I was billing that month. It wasn't so much the question that was asked that bothered me, but how it was asked and the motive behind it—he knew how much I was billing because I only had one client, and it wasn't enough to cover my wage, and he'd only asked the question to reiterate that point. It was something that we both knew, though, and he was making a statement about who held the power in our relationship.

From thereon in, I made it my goal to catch him up as quickly as possible, even though he was billing maybe five times as much as me at the start-up point. Perhaps he sensed this competitive behaviour of mine and it made him feel a certain way, ultimately causing a rift within our relationship. That was the impression I got.

I think the newness of everything carried us both through the first year, but in years two and three, I think we both just put our heads down and focused on our own agendas. I was trying to catch him up, and he was trying to stay ahead of me. We had built the firm up to about 10 staff, and they must have felt the tension most days. We tried to smile our way through the battle, but the staff were pulled from pillar to post every time either of us signed up a new client. Of course, we both thought our own clients were the most important!

People have told me in the past that I am a control freak, and I am not sure I agree, but I do acknowledge it has been said. I certainly wasn't in this instance. My business partner controlled all our access to management information records. I saw them rarely, didn't have much input on them, and was just concentrating on reaching our billing target. This proved to be a major error when we finally made the call to split up because it was only really then that it hit me, and maybe him—the actual position of our business. We owed an awful lot of money to creditors.

To be fair to him, he brought things to a head. One day, he came to me and said he had decided it was best for both of us if we called it a day, and he added that he was thinking of setting up on his own and taking his client base with him. We didn't have a shareholders agreement but we had a friendly enough chat to sort things out. Within a week, his website had gone live, he had moved out, notified his clients, and had also approached a number of our staff to join him!

At this point, we owed about £300k to creditors, if my memory is correct, and we agreed to split the debt equally between us, so Sedulo version 2.0's starting position was £150k in the hole. I had about £250k of revenue and £350k of costs, so my half of the debt was projected to grow at almost £10k per month. I kept the Sedulo name, but I also agreed to take on the lease we had at the time, since I had personally guaranteed it anyway.

I think perhaps the biggest contributor to our breakup was the difference in our personal lives. He was married with a son when we first started, while I had no children. All I had was Sedulo, and creating a successful business meant everything to me.

Now I look back, and I can accept why it didn't

work without blaming anyone—it was simply about timing. We had reached different stages in our lives, and our life plans were different as well, which suggests we should never have gone into business together in the first place.

Clearly, with a family to support, he had much larger outgoings than me, thus his focus was on short-term profitability while my focus was on long-term wealth growth. I wanted to take on staff. He wanted to earn more money. Neither of us were wrong—we just weren't aligned, and in hindsight, that's no one's fault.

Choose business partners wisely

My situation is not uncommon, and I see it time and time again within our client base.

You will often find situations, or might even currently be in a situation, where three people set up in business together—one has the idea and the drive, the other is more sales-focused, and the other, often the most organised of the three, looks after the back end. This seems like the perfect combination, with all bases covered. More often than not, it works at the start, during the "dating stage" when everything is new as was the case for us, but as the business develops, conflicting ideas between the parties start to emerge. And that's perfectly normal, of course, because within the first two years or so of running the business, they have realised what is and isn't working, and the business model is often dramatically different from the original plan.

We have advised on many business breakups involving three people, and what we usually notice is that two of the parties have formed more of an alliance.

On many occasions, there are no shareholder agreements in place, and this can make it much trickier, but in any case, in the end it comes down to the individuals involved and the amount of bad blood there is between them.

If it's not working, take decisive action

I often advise clients to break up sooner rather than later, which may seem like an extreme stance to take, but I just don't see the point in trying to make a business work if people are being distracted by internal politics, or if the organisation is clearly lacking direction because of differences in opinion at the top of the organisation. In circumstances such as these, breakup is inevitable in any case, but perhaps after years of damage to their business and their own personal lives—being part of a leadership team that's pulling in different directions is very stressful, especially for the staff caught up in it.

It doesn't even have to be *that* bad for a breakup to be for the best, and more often than not, there is a solution that is in the best interests of all partners to take forward. In my case, we have done well since, and no doubt the same could be said of my business partner. We don't speak any more only because we don't have a reason to, but we have never had an argument either—it was simply a case of wrong timing and wrong alignment of objectives.

If you're living the same situation today, work on regaining alignment with each other, and if that fails, try to find a mutually beneficial way out of it.

If at first you don't succeed...

My first attempt had kind of failed, not dramatically because I had built a client base and had some staff for my next venture. It had not put me off, either.

My new business was founded with an immediate debt of £150k inherited from the old company and a trading deficit of £10k per month. What did I do? Well, I got a further debt of £40k in the form of a bank overdraft, and to help the cash flow, my parents bought 10% of the business for £30k, and we were reborn.

I bought my parents back out a few years later for £75k, so the shares turned out to be a nice little investment for them—although they would have made substantially more by now if they had kept them!

Despite the fact that my first project had not gone according to plan, I would still not change anything, even though my own personal net liabilities, including my share of the old company's debt, were in the region of £200k. I had £10k equity in my house at that point.

I trusted my gut instinct to go again, and it's a really good job that I didn't over-analyse the situation because logic would have told me to pack it all in. My mind told me we could trade out of this. And the fear of having no other alternative meant we just had to. As I mentioned earlier, sometimes it's a great position to be in, to not have any other option.

Take action...

1. Agree on objectives

Many people end up in business with business partners. It's important to do this only with people who have common objectives—otherwise, it's going to impact on the business with mixed messages to the team. When you set out, make sure you have clear, aligned, individual objectives that can easily be translated into your business goals and targets.

2. If at first you don't succeed, go again

Very few entrepreneurs get it right first time, and none get it right all of the time, so it's likely that there will be failures along the way, and they are most common at the beginning whilst you have least experience. Don't let that put you off learning from these mistakes and going again.

Chapter VI

Have Clear Objectives

Have a business plan

I have mentioned that my first project probably didn't work because the objectives of the individuals involved, and therefore the resultant business objectives, were different and misaligned. I didn't make the same mistake twice.

I have to be honest here and say that if I had drawn up a written business plan to get out of the mess I found us in, I am not sure I could have conjured up one that would have made enough sense to push on with. For that sake I am glad, looking back, that I didn't have one.

Every business needs a concise plan—but I don't mean a written business plan. I have to admit that I have never written a business plan for Sedulo. Some people need them, but some people don't. I am one of those that don't.

We have clients who want to create something in writing at the start of every year that they can stick on their fridge as a daily reminder of their goals. It helps them to stay focused and I get that, and if that works for you, then do it.

Please don't make the mistake of thinking that I didn't have a plan—I just didn't have a *written* business plan. I could see where we were heading and what we needed to do with crystal clarity. I had a plan. My business plans, strange as this sounds coming from an accountant, are in my head or scribbled on bits of paper. Besides, even if I had written a business plan for each year, it would have changed 12 weeks in, and it would have become useless very quickly—such is the pace we are working at, in Sedulo.

That said, if having a written business plan provides you with the focus you need to keep reaffirming your journey, then you should do it.

Identify your business objectives

What I had, from day one, were clear business objectives that we wanted to achieve.

Do you ever find yourself in a position where your team seems to be constantly chasing its tail when it comes to making decisions, and more importantly, the implementation of decisions that were made? One of the biggest threats to businesses is a lack of clarity when it comes to decision-making.

I see clients, whether they are one-owner

businesses or ownership teams, making decisions with complete conviction only to then do an about-turn the very next day after a meeting. Two to three months on, they still haven't implemented any change and haven't made progress—it is one of the most frustrating parts, I guess, of being an advisor.

When we started out, it was to achieve the following objectives and they were very clear:

1 Create shareholder value by growing the business
2 Become a world-class employer
3 Create a world-class client experience
4 Maintain financial stability (there's the accountant again)

We set our goals, and we set about achieving them.

Once *you* have set *your* goals, and you need to stick to no more than three or four or they will probably conflict, concentrate on making decisions that take you closer to achieving them.

This is what we have always tried to do in Sedulo 2.0, but it's also what lead to most of the disagreements between my original business partner and me. I was fully focused on growth for long-term wealth—he wanted profit to sustain a lifestyle. I was entitled to my goals and he was entitled to his, but neither of us was ever going to move and that's why ultimately we didn't work as a partnership together. It doesn't mean either of us was more right than the other.

I think the final straw came in my original partnership when I wanted to recruit a relatively highly paid tax advisor to expand our service offering and chase further growth (and enhance our value). He wanted to keep the bottom line profit percentage at industry-standard rates.

Make the objectives as measurable as you can

Now, if you take another look at my business objectives, the first was to create shareholder wealth in the business. In order to do this, you must understand what the value of your business is and I am sometimes bewildered that clients come to see us without any clue of the value of their company. Do you know the value of yours? If not, go and find out—it's probably the most valuable asset you own. I have constantly measured the value of our business from day one.

I was very aware that accountancy firms are valued as a metric of their turnover, and this is typically 1–1.4 times annual revenue, so you could estimate Sedulo, for example, to be currently worth close to £10m. Over time, I therefore pushed turnover as you'd expect, seeing as I was focused on our wealth.

For clarity, businesses can be valued on many different variables, and are often valued as a multiplier of their EBITDA, revenue or even gross profit. Some are valued simply on the level of growth or the value of the data they own. It can be tricky to assess.

But if wealth is important to you, and the focus of your business is value, make sure you understand exactly what that value is.

Focus on cash!

Whilst I don't spend time on writing business plans, there is one thing I have complete focus on—cash. I have seen so many companies that have a great business on the surface, but underneath, have a business model that has a poor cash cycle. There is little chance for longevity in a business that operates like that, and in an industry like ours where you are doing the work, then invoicing customers to get paid for services in arrears, it's not the greatest business cash flow model.

My biggest fear, and your biggest fear should be, running out of cash. I'll talk later about how we have grown Sedulo organically, but how we also included a strategy of mixing the cash flow models of each new division to de-risk us from the traditional accountancy cash flow business model.

If ever I am interviewed about our story, I tend to get asked what I regret. The truth is that I regret nothing, I accept things I have done wrong and treat everything as a learning experience. What I learnt from my original partnership was that we focused on billing and invoicing rather than cash collection, and you have seen where that got us. I don't intend to make that same mistake twice.

I get a cash report every single day on the business. I have had coaching sessions where I have been told that I don't need to concentrate every day on cash. I chose to ignore that particular piece of advice.

Make decisions with complete clarity

Once you have a set of objectives that are crystal clear, the decision-making process should become more concise and less questionable. For the example I used earlier, in regard to a highly paid tax manager being the end of Sedulo version 1.0, I knew profit would suffer in the short term, but I also recognised that we would be able to do work we wouldn't otherwise be able to do at that time, so it would lead us towards our (my!) business objective of growth. It would also push us closer towards being able to offer a world-class service if we could offer high-level tax advice—a double whammy! A complicated decision was made easy for me.

Recognise what's important

I am a non-executive director of a client of ours in Manchester, an events company called Make Events owned by its founder, Holly Moore. It has a client base to die for, including the likes of Betfred, Vimto, Virgin, and The Hut Group. I have been a board advisor to Holly since 2018, and she will call me often when she has a key decision to make—it is sometimes a lonely place, running a business alone, as some of you will know.

During one visit, I asked Holly what was personally important to her, and she described the ideal home that she would like to buy. She went into detail about this house for two or three minutes, and then she stopped. I asked what else was important to her.

Holly then spent around 30 minutes talking about how she wished she had more time to travel and do the things she wanted to do, but how she couldn't because the business relied on her as it had no management structure in place at the time.

She explained how desperate she was for Make Events to become a well-recognised brand and how she would like to do a lot more public speaking to develop her own personal brand. She didn't have the time to do any of it.

Once she had gone through telling me about all the things she wanted to do but didn't have time for, I suggested that buying the house couldn't be the most important thing to her. She disagreed and reaffirmed that it was. In response to this, I said, 'Draw the money out of your business bank account then—today—and go and buy it!'

She didn't, although she had the money to, so clearly that wasn't really her most important goal because if it was, she would have done so.

Buying the house wouldn't have solved the other issues she had spoken so passionately about for half an hour, yet they were clearly the issues that were truly important to Holly. Taking the cash reserves from the business would have made the likelihood of achieving any of those other goals more remote. The fact that she had spent around 90% of her time with me that day speaking about those other objectives made me think they were the most important things to her—not the house!

If all those other things were the most crucial to Holly, it made more sense for her to put the house to one side and go about building a plan for a business that would give her the freedom to do what she wanted—which is exactly what she did.

By sticking to her plan, she would achieve her

most pertinent personal objectives, and following on from that, be able to buy that house further down the line. She is well on her way to achieving both goals.

Now that brings me on to a story that always sticks in mind…

Be more crayfish

A crayfish has a shell that protects it from the elements. As the crayfish grows, its shell doesn't. It reaches a point where the shellfish has to "shell" its protection in order to grow further. However, as soon as it has shelled its security, it immediately becomes exposed, vulnerable, and no doubt anxious.

There are various videos on YouTube that show the shelling process speeded up, and you can see the crayfish's anxiety very clearly in the way it physically reacts. It will immediately back up to find security where it can—if it's in a fish tank, it will back up into the corner, for example.

This is a great metaphor for what we must do constantly as business owners. Once we reach a position where we are comfortable in our shell, we have to push ourselves to the next level that requires exposing ourselves to risk.

We have to overcome this fear of fragility, exposure, and the unknown, in order to grow, but then over time, our shell regrows and we once again have our security blanket, but now we are much larger and stronger than we once were.

I have used this example to illustrate the point to many clients, and I indeed remind myself of the analogy whenever I am stepping the business up and feeling anxious about it.

Balance profitability with growth

I have always been focused on making millions rather than thousands—where that focus gets me, we shall see.

As soon as I discovered that the value of my wealth grew by the top line revenue figure, that became my focus. We didn't focus on profit, because it's very rare you can have it both ways. To get the top line, you need growth by reinvesting the profits back into the business, and this is what I have done all along.

You can't make £3m profit from £1m turnover—full stop—so my plan was always to reach a certain revenue figure that would allow us to drive the profit to a level we desired by tinkering with the costs. In an industry like ours, you can make £3m profit from £10m of revenue, so when Sedulo reaches a large enough size, perhaps we will switch our goal to focus on profit as opposed to growth—but for now, we need to speed past the £10m mark.

I have remained pretty focused, throughout our journey, with clearly defined goals, but I am going to tell you time and time again that the road to success does not follow a straight line of progress. Even with everything in place, a curveball will create havoc and uncertainty. When it does, you're going to have to be able to pivot sharply, adapt the plan, and dig deep.

Take action...

1. Focus on cash

The lifeblood of every business is not its profit or loss or balance sheet status, but its cash flow position in the short term, and the cash flow model of the business in the medium and long term.

Of all the reports you have within your business, the cash flow report is the most important.

2. Make decisions with complete clarity

Use your objectives to help you make quick decisions with complete clarity. I have clients who procrastinate over decision after decision because of a lack of crystal clear thinking.

As a result, competitors with a concise plan, carried out with conviction, can steal the market.

Chapter VII

Know Your Why

Even if you have the most clear, concise, written (or memorised!) business plan, you'd better be prepared for the journey. Because that business plan and those goals are going to change and end up looking very different, despite all that organisation and preparation.

You also need to understand there is a very fine line between success and failure. When you succeed, you will look back on the failures with a pride and a fondness. Not one of the successful people who I have interviewed has ever given an account that didn't include some time at the bottom of the ladder. The more adversity they have overcome, the more they beam with pride. Every one of them has one thing in common—resilience to succeed despite whatever adversity is thrown at them. Your why is going to give *YOU* that resilience.

When we set up Sedulo, I remember thinking

just a few years of hard work and I will be rich. No way would I have thought it would take me the length of time it has, and that's with pretty good growth too. In my industry, the average growth rate is usually around 10–15% per annum. Sedulo has been achieving significantly greater growth than this, and has grown by over 100% per annum for some of those years. Yet, it has still taken almost 10 years to achieve what I thought would take just two or three.

And I am as stressed today as I was starting out all those years ago because being in business is a constant battle to overcome challenges. As one challenge is overcome, another one presents itself. The challenges change, but it is mostly a case of swapping one problem for another.

It's bloody hard work being an entrepreneur, business owner or leader!

Knowing your why is a powerful tool

There is a clip on the internet, showing former undisputed world heavyweight champion boxer Mike Tyson fighting a rank outsider—a 40/1 underdog called James "Buster" Douglas. The fight took place in 1990, when Tyson was widely considered as the fiercest man on the planet. He had knocked out almost every opponent that had stepped in the ring with him.

The fight was going to plan when Tyson typically knocked Douglas down in the eighth round, only for the challenger to be saved by the bell. On every other occasion leading up to this fight, Tyson had stopped each his opponents pretty soon after putting them on the canvas. This time, however, things didn't go according to the script.

Douglas rose from his corner and took the fight to Tyson—he believed he could do what no one else could. He fought back, and in what is considered one of the biggest upsets in sporting history, he stopped Tyson in the tenth round. The sporting world was stunned. The unstoppable had been stopped.

When asked how, on earth, he had managed such a feat, Douglas simply replied, 'Because of my mother…God bless her heart.'

The story goes that his mother had died two days before the fight, having told everyone that her son was going to beat Mike Tyson, and Douglas was determined to make his mother's dream a reality. The strength of his why completely overrode everything else on the night, and that why gave him the inner belief, even while sat on the canvas in the eighth round, that he was going to get up and he was going to beat Tyson. The mind will make you quit before your body will.

Learn that your why changes over time

In a podcast interview with the chairman of JD Sports, Peter Cowgill, I asked what his why was. The first thing he spoke about was how he had seen his parents fight over a chocolate bar when he was a young child.

He had decided there and then that he would never let that happen to him. That had been his primary motivator, and it is interesting that just as I do, he had immediately traced back his why to a childhood event.

Something similar happened when I interviewed

Jason Rickaby, co-founder of sports nutrition brand PhD Nutrition, for another podcast. He remembered his mum and dad arguing over money and how he had vowed that this would never happen to him.

It's pretty clear in Cowgill's case, though, heading up such a successful business as JD Sports plc, which has recently been valued at £5 billion that he no longer has to worry who is sharing the last Kit Kat in the house.

But he's still going for success at a ferocious pace, and he describes it as a drug. Working hard, achieving results, feeding his own ego in his own words, is the daily drug that he needs.

'When will you quit?' I asked him.

'When I can get off the drug—end of story!' he replied without hesitation, so clearly his why has evolved over time.

I have often been asked what my why is, and in truth, it's a difficult one to answer because I always thought it had changed over time. More recently, I have come to terms with where my deeper drive originates.

When I set out, I was a single guy with no children. My why—created all that time ago in a mechanics garage in Stockport—was, simply put, because I wanted a better life. It started right at home—it was all about me. Not that I was selfish...

I would like to think that people close to me would say I am a very generous person—giving to others is something I pride myself on—but I think you can give more to others, and I don't just mean financially, when you yourself are in a good place, be it mentally, spiritually or financially.

The truth is, no matter what tangible possessions

I gained, I didn't feel any sense of achievement and still felt as driven as ever to achieve more. This often left me feeling confused, and down in many ways, seeing that every time I arrived at my destination, the reality of it fell short of the expected satisfaction.

I can only think that, unknown to me until now, all this time I have had a subliminal desire to be accepted rather than rejected as I had been as a child. Being successful in business made me feel accepted, giving back to the people does too, and I guess that's why I feel as though I am on a one-man crusade to do just that—after I have secured the future of my family, of course.

I read a book called *The Subtle Art of Not Giving a F*ck* by Mark Manson, which I recommend you read as well if you haven't already. It was while I was reading that book that I also realised more about myself.

A big why of mine is to leave a legacy, and it is driven by another deep fear—death.

We are all going to die at some point, and if I think about that for any period of time, it scares the absolute shit out of me. It completely unnerves me—it is the one thing we can't control and I have a severe problem with that for some reason. I have not managed to conquer this fear as yet.

Leaving a legacy is the only way to outlive my death, and it provides me with comfort that *maybe I won't die on my deathbed after all!*

So my why is to create that legacy in as many ways as I can—through my wife and kids, my businesses, and by making the biggest impact on this world that little old me possibly can.

This is all still work in progress to me, and I haven't found the definitive answer. I am still searching. Whilst it was all worrying at first, and a complete mindfuck if I am truly honest, I am now embracing the process of self-awareness—you should too.

Give something back

I move with urgency to make an impact on the community around me, and to help cement that legacy. Is it all so I can feel accepted?

Sedulo has a community arm, and I take great pleasure in seeing how much we do within our local environment. From supporting charities to helping in schools, we try to contribute, and we even designed and created an inspiring workspace within my old school.

Every Christmas, we organise a "Santa's grotto" where we provide presents and gifts for over 200 children, who would otherwise get nothing at Christmas time. I'd like to think this is a selfless act, but it's not. It makes me feel good, and I am not sure there is anything wrong with that—it's a win-win.

I try to give back to my old school, as I mentioned before. I give talks to the children there, and just recently we created a "reward room" for good behaviour. It's a room where the kids who have worked hard for that week can go enjoy a range of features, including a New York-style apartment area for watching television programmes and an indoor lawn area with a table tennis table. You will see where these themes have come from later on.

I am also very fortunate to be the chair of a very

special charity called Once Upon a Smile.

Once Upon a Smile is a children's bereavement charity, set up by friends and actors Daniel Jillings and Danny Miller that focuses on families where there has been a tragedy. There might have been a sudden death in the family or one of the children might have sadly passed away after a long-term illness.

Often, the long-term illness of one of the kids will bring huge changes in the family's circumstances. As you'd expect, the parents shift all their focus towards the child who is sick. Work becomes a secondary consideration, leading to a decline in the family's financial situation.

The "well" siblings must go through a traumatic time wondering why their brother or sister is getting all the attention and why *Mummy and Daddy are always upset*. This goes on until one day, they have to figure out why their sick sibling is no longer around. Once Upon a Smile focuses on the siblings who remain after the tragic passing.

We provide financial assistance to help these families get back on their feet. We also pay for respite breaks for them to reintegrate with one another, but by far the most required services are the bereavement groups and classes for children that were set up especially for the same purpose.

Once Upon a Smile is a registered charity and I love being chair of it, although if I am honest, I wish I could give it more time and one of my goals is to do just that now that Sedulo has reached the stage that it has.

I wouldn't have had the opportunity to make these contributions for the greater good had it not been for my business career, and I wouldn't have had the drive to have the business career I have without my why—they go hand in hand.

And I am most certainly not alone. As a working-class guy, my Facebook includes friends from all walks of life, and I am pretty quick to defend against the "rich don't give a fuck about the poor" type posts when I see them because I have never found that to be remotely true in my experience.

We have a client base that constantly gives back to society, and I would like to think that's the norm—because once you have enough to look after your dearest, what else is there to do?

So what's yours?

I know I keep repeating this, but you know all those social posts you've seen, showing business owners setting up their companies and then taking pictures of their cappuccinos next to their Macs whilst chilling on the beach? Yes, them—you've seen them! Well, it's not all like that. In fact...

It's far fucking from it!

And when you're wondering how on earth you're going to get through it and continue your life as an entrepreneur, when you are on the floor just as Buster Douglas was in his fight, your why is going to kick in and push you through barrier after barrier.

If you have found yours, well done. If you haven't, I am going to give you a little tip...

Don't think it's just about numbers

Equating your why to numbers is always a problem because, as I am sure you will have experienced yourself, the numbers are never enough. You want to earn £x, you earn it—then, within a month or so, you find that £x isn't enough.

If your driver for achievement is based on hitting numbers, the likelihood is that you will never feel content because the numbers will just keep moving as you hit them. I made this mistake for years!

I remember a time when my target was to make sure I was earning £1k per year for every year I had lived. That was one of my first measurements of success; i.e. by the age of 25, I wanted to be earning £25k per year. I hit that, and within weeks I wanted £30k per year; *now <u>that</u> would be an achievement*, I thought—until I hit it, and then I wanted more again. Nothing has changed on that front. We have all been there.

When I started the business, I used to tell Lee Jones, one of my business partners in Sedulo version 2.0, 'When we get to £30k a month revenue, we have made it, mate. Keep going.' We worked 80–100 hours a week until we got there...and then we wanted £50k per month in revenue.

Not long ago, I saw an internal report that said we were expected to make £50k profit in one month, and it wasn't enough, because we had expected to hit more. Seven years earlier, I had thought I would feel on top of the world if we could earn *that* in monthly revenue, and now we were making that amount in *profit!* And I still wasn't happy!

I'm not alone, and I am sure you will all recognise this trait exists within most of us. On the recent podcast I did with Jason Rickaby, of PhD Nutrition, he was talking about how he had recently sold out, and I asked him how he felt on the exit. Surprisingly, it was the biggest anti-climax ever. He said it was like any other day, and it certainly wasn't how he had expected it to be. Numerous people have said the same.

I did a deal not long ago where one of my clients took £5m off the table for a part of his business. We signed the documents, he ordered an Uber, and then he went home to have a cup of tea with his wife. It was like any other day.

How do you define your success?

I have already stated that I personally find it difficult to associate myself with being successful.

I have also spoken about how other successful individuals never equate their success to a certain figure. To find out what success is to you, and to discover your driver, you need to go much deeper than this.

What I urge you to do is to embrace this journey of self-realisation, whatever that looks like for you because your journey is unique to you.

In the beginning, I thought these thoughts and this confusion were nothing but a headfuck and a nuisance, but if you take time to understand what you want, you won't feel disappointed with yourself for your lack of happiness when you achieve your "goals".

No one wants to have a £10m turnover business but be a crap dad. If you get to £10m turnover and think you're a crap dad, guess what? You're not going to be satisfied, so search deeper than that.

I have been grappling with this question throughout the time I have been in business, and I can say that I have a better grasp of it now that I ever did previously, although I don't know all the answers. What I didn't realise in my earlier years was just how painful a process it would be mentally…

Take action...

1. Give something back

Almost everybody I have interviewed for the podcasts maintain a high level of motivation, long after they have achieved personal financial success, by doing things for others. Done as part of a team, it can generate a great camaraderie amongst your staff. Remember to give back to things that are close to them, too.

2. Make sure you measure your success with achievements that are greater than numbers

If you define your success in numbers, it's likely you will never feel a great sense of achievement. I mention repeatedly in this book that as soon as you hit your target, you will move the goalposts and be on with the next one. To define your success, try to find things that give a greater sense of achievement—such things usually focus around relationships.

Chapter VIII

Learn to Cope With Stress

I remember it as clear as day. I had nipped out to grab a rare sandwich for lunch. For weeks, I had not been feeling myself. It hadn't been anything too serious, just the occasional spell of light-headedness, and sometimes I'd experienced what I can only describe as speckled, blurred vision.

After a short drive through the local village to the sandwich shop, I stepped out of my car, but as I started to walk, I felt a wave of something coming over me. I tried to take a few steps more, but my legs began to feel increasingly heavy until they reached the point where I couldn't get them to function. It was as though I had blocks of stone where my feet should have been, and I was feeling physically sick. By this time, I had started to sweat profusely. Something was wrong. My mind was racing, trying to compute what was going on.

Am I having a heart attack?

Am I about to die?

Right now? In the street?

Fuck me, it wasn't supposed to end like this! I still have far too much to do!

My heart was beating so hard, it was almost bursting out of my chest, and my stomach was churning. And then it happened…

There was no warning, and it was instant.

My energy just left my body. At the time, I wondered whether it was energy or life itself that was draining from me. It was as if a giant vacuum had come along and was just taking it.

FUCK!

I couldn't get any breath into my lungs. My throat and chest were just so tight. I remember thinking *I am pretty fit, I am in good shape, I am a 28-year-old guy, for fuck's sake. How, on earth, can I be dying in a street—what the fuck is wrong with me?*

It also felt embarrassing. I don't know what came over me, or how I did it, but I managed to trudge to the nearest shop, a supermarket, and I bought a tabloid newspaper. There was a bench outside, and if I could just get to it and lie down, I might recover from this. The newspaper was to cover my face in case anyone saw me.

That was the plan.

I made it to the bench and fell asleep. Or had I died? At the time, I really didn't know.

Try not to panic

Thankfully, I woke up, took a deep breath, and felt the sun's heat on my skin. At least I wasn't dead. The feeling of relief that came over me was overwhelming, and I felt like crying. My next thought, ridiculously at the age of 28—*I want Mum!* I didn't know what I wanted her for. I just needed her. I got myself together and summoned enough energy to make it back to the motor, where I sat down and closed my eyes. *What is up with me?* I wondered. *This can't be right.*

Mum was at home when I called. That's all I needed to know. I started the engine. Now, I had lived in the family home from being born until the age of 26, so it would always feel special to me, a place where I could recharge. Within seconds of getting there, I was laid on the sofa.

I explained that I wasn't feeling well, and Mum made me a piece of toast, I think, before I nodded off. When I woke up again, I wouldn't say I'd made a full recovery, but I felt a billion percent better than I had before. I just felt comforted by the surroundings.

My mum thought I'd just had a funny turn, she didn't have a clue what had actually happened and how intense it had been.

Unfortunately, the symptoms started all over again just a few days later. This time, I took myself back to my own house to try to sleep it off. But it didn't work. As soon as I woke up, I started to feel worse. I remember needing the toilet, but unlike the last episode when I had been able to walk into the shop, I was now so lacking in energy and feeling so heavy, that I had to drag myself across the floor like some kind of mermaid. I effectively had no legs!

This time I am definitely dying, I concluded.

I reached for the phone, dialled 999 and asked to be put through to the ambulance service.

'Come and help me. I'm dying,' I pleaded. 'I think I'm having a heart attack.'

I was in a state of complete panic. My breathing was short and fast, and it felt like I was being strangled. To my horror, the lady on the other end of the phone said she didn't think it was a heart attack, and I would have to make my own way to the A & E department. This heightened my panic. 'I am going to fucking die,' I spat, exasperated. 'I can't walk, let alone drive!'

The woman on the end of the phone tried her

best to assure me that it wasn't a heart attack, but her words weren't getting through. I was so scared and angry. *How could she leave me to die when I have called for help!*

To be fair to the lady, now that I have the benefit of hindsight, I realise that she has probably had to deal with many a similar call to mine before—so she recognised it was a panic attack, not a heart attack, and I did manage to make it to A & E on my own! As I said earlier, your mind will give up before your body.

Not long after arriving, I was seen by the triage nurse, but then I had to sit in a waiting room for a couple of hours. During the second hour, I nearly went ballistic at the nurses. I remember thinking, *I'm going to fucking die in the waiting room and people are coming in with trivial injuries.*

They finally called me into a consultation room where they carried out a few checks and gave me an ECG scan. Everything was fine! As soon as I was given the all-clear by the medics, the energy and life flooded back into my body as quickly as it had left, with one powerful wave.

The doctor explained that I was stressed. I didn't get it. 'What do you mean, I am stressed? I feel fine,' I protested, and I genuinely thought I was. My mind was playing tricks on me, and I didn't like it at all.

It was a frightening period of my life. I went on to experience three or four further episodes over the next six months, and on each occasion, I wouldn't recover until I was sitting with the doctor and hearing him or her tell me that I was going to be okay.

If you have ever been in this position, just know that you're not on your own. The worst part for me, when I experienced these panic attacks, was not being able to control my actions. Losing control over what the body is doing is the scariest thing in the world. Perhaps I am a control freak, after all. I remember thinking I was going crazy, that I couldn't control my thoughts, and wondering where it was all going to end—and that scared me further. It is a very vicious circle, and you can easily find yourself spiralling downwards quickly when you're in that state of mind.

Lots of questions that I had never thought about before entered my head:

> *What if I can't control my thoughts, and this gets worse—can it get worse?*
> *Why am I the only person in the world who thinks like this?*
> *Will they come and section me if this doesn't stop?*
> *Am I depressed?*
> *Am I crazy?*

Again, if you have ever felt like this and found yourself having these thoughts, now you know you are not alone.

I am happy to discuss my battle with anxiety because the worst part is feeling as though you are the only one experiencing these thoughts and feelings. The truth is that you're not, none of us are that special, and you can guarantee that whatever thoughts you're having, there are millions of others going through the same experience. So why not talk about it?

I soon realised that this issue would never leave me, and that led to the natural conclusion that I would have to learn to live with it and control how I deal with my fears, which is exactly what I have done.

As I became better at observing how my mind worked, I discovered what was triggering my feelings of anxiety. It had nothing to do with the past or the present moment. The problem only arose when I was thinking about something that was possible in the future, even if that possibility was remote.

I have read somewhere that dwelling on the past is more likely to lead to a depressive state, but I have never suffered this particular problem, given that I have a strong tendency to live mostly in the future.

I chatted to former Team Great Britain athlete, Commonwealth gold medallist and Olympian Diane Modahl MBE, not so long ago. Her podcast interview was different than many of my others for one reason—when she talked about her achievements, she talked so much about living in the moment. The touch, the smell, the sense of pride she felt at each milestone.

It was unusual to listen to someone, who at the height of their success, lived for that moment, and you could see in her demeanour that she was almost back there when she spoke. I can also tell you that, in general, Diane came across as a much more mentally considered and calm individual, at least on the surface, than most that I speak to. Certainly more so than me!

Learn to live with anxiety

Now that I had gained a little more insight into the root of my anxiety, I was determined to find ways of dealing with it, and I'm going to share some of these methods with you.

Firstly, I accepted that I was prone to the problem and it wasn't going to go away by itself. This was a *big* breakthrough for me—it meant that instead of feeling scared of the state of anxiety itself, I began to see it as a sign that something needed to be addressed and action needed to be taken.

Secondly, I educated myself on the subject and found out that a panic attack, whilst being frightening, is actually one of the body's self-protection mechanisms that have evolved over the 200,000 years that humans have been around.

For our ancient ancestors, fear was the difference between avoiding a dangerous situation and living to tell the tale or falling victim to misfortune. For modern man, most of our threats are not as tangible as the bears of the forest or the sabretooth tigers that our ancestors had to face in the past. They tend to be psychological, but the body reacts to them just as though they were another predator about to pounce.

Panic attacks themselves are not unusual and there would be nothing odd about someone having one or two in their lifetime. It is when they happen more frequently, as was happening to me, that they become an issue.

By the way, the human body can't stay in a state of panic for longer than 60 minutes so when you think it will never end, try to remember that your body will bring itself out of the attack within an hour—so I am told. For many people, their attacks are gone within 20 minutes. A huge part of my ability to cope with anxiety came from accepting that a panic attack is meant to save you, not hurt you. If you suffer from attacks, get to grips with this concept.

Having acknowledged and accepted that I had this problem and having found out a little more about the disorder, I had to decide how I was going to tackle it, and I made up my mind that—if possible—I was going to beat it without the use of medication.

I have very rarely taken tablets for anything, always preferring to allow nature to take its course for headaches, upset stomachs or other forms of general ill health. Where there is a problem, there has to be a source, and I believe it is better to find that and tackle it rather than using medication to block out the symptoms.

I am not qualified to tell you what to do if you find yourself experiencing panic attacks or any other episode of ill health, but I am going to highlight some of the natural steps, which I've started taking, that have benefitted my mental and physical health. They may work for you.

Let go of your thoughts

I had read somewhere that the legendary boxing trainer Cus D'Amato had encouraged his protégé, Mike Tyson, with these words: 'Your mind is not your friend, Mike. I hope you know that. You have to fight with your mind. Control it. Put it in its place.' I spent the first few years absorbing this advice and fighting my mind. The problem was that I got tired of fighting. It was hard work being constantly at war with my own mind.

I read somewhere else that the Buddhist approach to disturbing intrusive thoughts is simply to notice them, let them pass and move on with life. Sounds easy,

I know, but I am being honest with you now—when I grasped this very simple thought process and stopped beating myself up about those intrusive thoughts, it was a game changer. I accepted them and moved on, and that required far less energy than the daily battle I was used to having with myself before.

Now, if I get a negative thought, I picture it as a cloud in the centre of my mind, and I wait for it to pass. Then I get on with the rest of my day.

Learn to control the controllable

One of the main causes of stress or anxiety is allowing your mind to wander. I look at it like a worry chain, a series of links that you formulate in your mind, that starts with an actual problem but soon ends up being a whole heap of problems.

Not long ago, I had a client come to me with a problem. His business was in slight regression, and it was nothing major, but to him it was.

He started by saying the company's culture was being destroyed by an individual within the team. I told him to get rid of the individual. He went on to explain that if he did this, then the dissenting individual's friend, who was critical to the business, would also leave.

Furthermore, he thought that their manager, who was also critical to the business, would leave as well, and the knock-on effect would be that turnover would plummet. This plummeting turnover would lead to them having to downsize and move out of their current office, and as they were known in their industry, everyone would find out they were struggling. As a result, they wouldn't be able to back recruit the leavers, and the business would almost capitulate. This was his worry chain. I think we have all been there, and we have all done this at some point.

I told the client the only thing he could guarantee, out of all the possibilities above, was that he had a problem with a member of staff, and he could control that by legitimately getting rid of the problem. He couldn't control anything beyond that since none of it may happen in any case. If it did, then he would have to deal with it at that point.

If you find yourselves in similar circumstances, try and remember to simply control that which is in your control, and make the decision with clarity. There is no point worrying about what you can't control.

Get some rest

The body needs time to recover, which it does when you stop running around, so make sure you are getting adequate rest during the day and enough quality sleep during the night.

This was an easy one for me because I have always been able to sleep pretty well, regardless of the amount of stress I've tended to be under. Then again, I perform with such ferocious intensity for the 16 hours I am awake, that I will usually fall asleep within 30 seconds of my head touching the pillow.

Do what you can to get yourself eight hours of sleep each night. There are a million studies out there that show how sleep leads to better performance in the workplace whilst providing excellent health benefits. I have noticed a massive correlation between how much or little sleep I get and my general level of anxiety. When I am not getting enough sleep, I am definitely more anxious.

If you haven't invested in a fitbit device, give one a try. Zeri bought me one as a Christmas present to help with my anxiety and sleep. It is a watch that synchronises with an application that gives you information about your heart rate, and importantly, your sleeping patterns.

It has the ability to collect information on what sleep phases you experience and when—light, deep and rapid eye movement (REM). By gaining greater understanding of such measurements, you have the power to make better lifestyle choices and improve your general health.

Stay hydrated

This is one of the simplest health practices you can do, but so many people neglect it, so make sure you don't. The body is made up of around 60% water, on average, with the brain and heart being composed of 73% water, for example, and even bone being a surprising 30% water[4].

Water is a vital nutrient for every cell in our bodies and is a necessary component for the building of new cells. We have billions of them! It is important for regulating our temperature, helping the carbohydrates and proteins that our bodies need to be metabolised and transported in the bloodstream, flushing out our system,

---

4 H.H. Mitchell, Journal of Biological Chemistry

protecting our brain and other vital organs from shock, making saliva, and lubricating joints.

No wonder we need so much of it!

It doesn't make sense for me not to ensure my body has enough water for optimal performance. There are some people around the world who have to walk for 20 miles just to reach water. We have it on tap and yet some of us are not drinking enough. Madness!

Ideally, a healthy person should consume around 2–3 litres of water every day, depending on their gender, size etc., but the recommended intake is 1.5 litres per day as a minimum. It is a quick and easy win, so water is now included as part of my daily routine. If I start to feel the "jitters" creeping up, one of the first things I will do is to take a seat and hydrate.

Make sure you exercise

Find something physical that you enjoy doing. The physical and psychological effects of exercise are so important.

I have trained or played sport my whole life, and I tend to work out almost every day, with one or two rest days per week. One of my friends is former European and British boxing champion John Murray, who used to be a pretty formidable fighter in his day, going on to become a world title challenger. I am fortunate enough to get to train with John on a regular basis, but I also mix up my boxing sessions with some runs, which help me to connect with nature and recharge myself.

I bang on the odd podcast every now and then, which is a great way to learn whilst enjoying the physical benefits of the exercise. The occasional weight training session adds variety and relaxes me because it's slightly less strenuous than the boxing sessions.

When I feel anxious or stressed, I only train moderately. I learnt that training too hard when your body is under pressure from other sources can actually make matters worse. So if I am feeling great, I will train hard, and if I don't feel so great, I will lower the intensity level.

There was a time when exercise was adding to my stress and anxiety. I was trying too hard to get to the gym to train, running into the gym whilst I was on the phone, still working whilst getting changed, and then finishing the call and jumping straight into a high-intensity workout that my body had not prepared for.

Now, if I have so much on at work that I will be creating stress just to fit a training session in, I simply don't bother. Almost all of my clients train. Some prefer the high-intensity stuff, and others enjoy their long walks to clear the mind. Find whatever works best for you, but do something you enjoy.

Eat well

This is the part I find most challenging because I like my coffee in the morning, and with the amount of socialising I do with work, I do tend to drink a fair amount of alcohol a couple of times a week. When you also bear in mind that I am running around most of the day, so the car is my office, and almost all "quick grab" food on the go is full of simple carbohydrates or refined sugar, it's easy to see how eating healthily is something that requires a conscious effort.

Given my lifestyle, my diet is far from perfect, particularly at the weekend with having three boys, but if I feel some of the symptoms of headaches, stomach flips or general nervousness coming on, I immediately stop or cut down on caffeine, alcohol and refined sugars as a first line of defence.

I am also monitoring my diet generally as I get older, to make sure I eat more of the correct stuff—I don't eat any carbohydrate-based foods in the morning or evening anyway because I try to use most of the day to burn fat as fuel, and to keep burning fat as a source you have to eat fat and not carbohydrates, so I am told.

I have no idea how things like refined sugars affect levels of anxiety, but I do listen to my body, and when I cut simple and refined sugars out of my diet, I seem to be in a generally healthier and better mood.

Making a conscious effort to monitor and balance my life in terms of rest, hydration, exercise and diet has helped me to keep stress and anxiety at bay, allowing me to live a normal life, even whilst operating mostly in high-pressure and stressful environments.

You are meditating, right?

If the answer to this question is "no", and you have been experiencing any of the symptoms of suffering from mental pressure, please do one thing when you put this book down—start meditating.

I read about anxiety being a form of energy that projects itself forward of the body because some of us are always thinking ahead in advancing and progressive situations. That makes a lot of sense to me. I once booked a group session that was being ran by a lady called Nikki Owen, an expert in the field of charisma and confidence. She measured my "aura field" and told me that it was emanating way ahead of my body. This kind of thing may sound a little hard to believe for some, but it's good to have an open mind, and Nikki is well respected within her field, often called upon by the media to provide comment or insight.

Nikki was also able to spot my anxiety from the minute I walked into the room, by noticing small physical tell-tale signs such as the disruption under my eyes that she said was directly related to anxiety within my stomach, and the forward projection of my neck ahead of my shoulders.

They say you learn something new every day, and if you ever get a chance to attend one of Nikki's lectures, I thoroughly recommend that you do. She had a lasting effect on me.

During the same session, Nikki asked us who meditated. There were around 20 of us in the room, and needless to say, every hand went up except for mine. I was also the youngest by at least five years, maybe 10. When I realised that all these people, who were older and more experienced than me, were all tapping into the same resource, I knew I had to give it a try.

From that night onwards, I set about finding out more about meditation. Every evening, I put aside 15 minutes to sit quietly and meditate with the aid of a guided meditation video on YouTube.

It is difficult to quantify exactly how much effect meditation has had on me, but I can tell you it's benefitting me enough to know that I won't take the chance of removing it from my life.

So if there is one thing you can take from this book, it's this—if you are struggling with any signs or symptoms of suffering due to anxiety, mental pressure or stress, and you are not meditating already, you need to introduce it into your life as a daily habit, starting now.

I try to measure my mental anxiety levels every day. There are few times that I'd say it exceeds what I would call a "three out of 10" level, but if it does, I kick in *all* the control mechanisms I have to bring it back down. I don't try a few and see how it goes. I won't and I don't take that chance.

If you suffer from mental illness, trust me there are things you can do to live a normal life without it consuming your thoughts. You have to take action and focus on your lifestyle choices, which means focusing on maintaining a healthy work-life balance.

Take action...

1. Learn to live with anxiety and stress

Anxiety is a mindset. It is a way of viewing and dealing with a certain situation. If you suffer from it, learn to turn it to your advantage. When we were cavemen, it used to save our lives by forcing us to remove ourselves from a potentially dangerous situation. Top performers will use the feelings associated with anxiety to sharpen their focus, to drive them forward.

2. Learn to control the controllables

Most sleepless nights are caused by creating scenarios in your head, of things that could happen—but never actually do! What a waste of time it is, worrying about things that are never going to happen. Break it down and deal with that which is happening and you have the ability to change the outcome. Ignore everything else and let the thoughts pass.

Chapter IX

Find a Healthy Work-life Balance

How often do you ask yourself *is my work-life balance right?*

Me? I've spent the last 10 years asking myself that question, and if I'm being honest, it's another thing I haven't got the answer for.

I have spent most of my thirties building the business, whilst becoming a father to three boys and trying in vain to be the best husband, father, son, friend, colleague, and person I can possibly be. It often seems like an impossible task, and sometimes it feels as though I am spread so thinly that none of the people I care about get to see enough of me.

If you're anything like me, you probably can't tell the difference between what is work and what is life. When I was given the opportunity to give a speech at my old school's end of year award ceremony in 2018, I tried to persuade the students that whatever they went on to do, they should choose something they had a genuine interest in.

If they are very lucky, they may get to do something they love. If you love what you do, how can it be classed as work? I don't believe I have done a day's work for well over 10 years. To get the business off the ground in the early years, though, I would "work" 16-hour days, seven days a week, including Christmas Day—and I loved every minute of it, so where's the problem?

I think technology has a huge part to play. Maybe I am being presumptuous here, but I am still old enough to remember a time when if I wanted to call someone, I had to find myself some coins and go to the local shop where I'd have to wait—often in the freezing cold, outside the public phone box—for the person in front of me to finish their call. Sometimes there was a queue! To make matters more unpleasant, phone boxes were also the place for groups of kids to shelter from the rain, or they were just something else for the local vandals to get stuck into, and I would then find myself tricked into picking up a handset that was covered in chewing gum.

As grim as all that sounds, when I reflect on what it would have been like to be running a business in those days, when communication channels were limited, I realise that at least it must have been possible to come home from work and focus on whatever you had planned for the evening—as opposed to being bombarded with phone calls, emails, texts, Whatsapp messages, and notifications from LinkedIn and Facebook, which has now become the norm for most of us.

Our personal channels have become business channels, and the lines have become blurred.

So what can you do about it?

When you give your time, *give* your time

When you *are* with your family, are you really *with* them…or do you find yourself picking up the phone and scrolling through your notifications? Is your mind elsewhere, thinking about the next list of endless business tasks that need completing?

If we are brutally honest with ourselves, this is an area many of us *do* need to work on. Let's not allow the muddy line between work and life to become so fuzzy that we think we are giving our time to our families when our heads are actually in our iPhones!

Someone once told me, 'If you are in the room, be *in* the room,' and that means putting devices away for a start so as not to be distracted, giving the people you love meaningful access to you.

Make it count for them

Looking back, I think I was deeply affected by the loss of my grandad when I was just 13 years old. I felt, and still feel, that he was taken too early because he missed out on so much of what I have done since. I have always had a burning desire to make my parents proud. After everything they have done for me, I think it's the least they deserve.

On the one hand, I am proud that, through my achievements, I have been able to show them there is more to life and broadened their horizons. Yet, I also feel an anxiety within me, urging me to develop at breakneck speed just so Mum and Dad can see me reach my full potential before it's too late. The irony is that they just want to spend more time with their son!

So when it comes to the people who matter, try to understand and appreciate what *they* want, not what you want.

I remember when I was a kid with Dad in his lorry, I used to spend all my school holidays driving around the UK with him. He was a keen boxing fan, and a big fight was about to take place in Las Vegas. Dad mentioned something about how great it would be to take me to a fight out there. At the time, I must have been around 10 years old, but it stuck with me for almost 20 years, and at the age of 29—the first time I made some money—I booked tickets so dad and I could fly out to watch the Ricky Hatton versus Floyd Mayweather Junior fight at the MGM in Las Vegas.

I did a similar thing for my mum when I booked tickets for the two of us to have dinner on the Northern Belle, a sister train of the Orient Express. We spent three hours together, just the two of us, sat opposite each other and talking. If you haven't done anything like this before, do it as soon as you can—when else do you get to spend one-on-one time with the person who brought you into the world? If you're anything like me, the answer will sadly be almost never.

Mix business with pleasure

I am very lucky, as I have said earlier, to have such an amazing array of clients, and it allows me to have access to things and experiences that would otherwise most likely be unreachable. My eldest son, Ethan, loves WWE, and I got to know one of the main stars, Wade Barrett, who is known in the ring as "Bad News Barrett".

Wade is a really great guy, and as a thank you to some of my fashion clients for dressing him, he said he would get us front row tickets at all the big UK events. I must have earned some brownie points from Ethan when we were sat in the front row at an event featuring the legendary "Undertaker"—but I must admit that, for a man of 38 years old, I got a little too excited!

I always have one eye on signing clients that can not only bring something to our business, but will also allow me leverage to give back to my family. It's a privilege to work with fashion clients such as Gok Wan, Forever Unique and Missy Empire, amongst others, and I am pretty sure this scores me enough points with Zeri for me to be able to attend event after event without any complaints from her!

We were very fortunate, when we got married, to be able to call upon our connections to celebrate our day. We had a "Nikki Beach" wedding!

Nikki Beach, for those of you who have never been, is a luxury beach club, which has resorts all around the world, and Zeri and I have been to many, but we brought it to Cheshire for our special day, complete with crisp white sofas, four-poster beds, shisha pipes, and live musicians in the form of saxophonists, bongo players and violinists.

We were also very privileged that performing for us on our day were chart-toppers Michelle Heaton of pop band Liberty X, BRIT award-winner Shola Ama, Angie Brown of dance group Bizarre Inc, and the amazing dance duo of Phats and Small.

Plenty of clients were in attendance, and I had a memorable day watching my oldest friends mixing with the celebrity guests in attendance and enjoying each other's company.

Even on my wedding day, you see, there was very little distinction between work and life—being an entrepreneur, one blends into the other.

Give yourself a break

It is important to consider what others want, but don't be so busy thinking about what other people want that you lose focus on what you want. Don't beat yourself up by over analysing your performance as to what you think other people's expectations of you are. As I mentioned earlier, I think my mum and dad want me to be more and more successful, but the reality is that they don't. They just want me to be happy and to spend more time with me and my family. If you look at yourself, I bet you're right at the back of the queue when it comes to giving yourself time. Well, if there is another important point you should take from reading this book, it is to make time for you.

You have to spend time on you, and you have to self-develop and self-progress. Even writing this book has enabled me to become more self-aware. The reflection process, that it has forced upon me, has made me analyse things slightly differently than I used to.

I have my issues, as we all do. Of late, I have learnt to accept my issues rather than look at myself with a critical eye. If I am insecure, so be it—perhaps early childhood trauma has forced that upon me. I don't dwell on it anymore, and I don't let it worry me. In fact, nowadays I embrace it, and I turn that negative into a positive. I have mentioned already that me being rejected as a child is possibly, maybe even probably, the thing that gives me the determination to succeed today, so maybe being insecure isn't that bad after all!

As I also discussed in one of the earlier chapters, giving to others starts with you. You have to put yourself on a solid footing. You can't give true love if you don't love yourself, you can't provide security to others if you're not secure yourself, and you can't provide a healthy environment for others if you're ill yourself, so it's down to you to work on a healthy work-life balance.

Make a list of things that are important to you, and put a plan in place to start doing them.

Step out of your comfort zone

It's so tempting when you start to do well at something to keep doing that over and over again, and to be honest, I am an advocate of this—it's part of the success journey. However, there are also times when you need to do something different, stretch yourself for your own self-progression, and to stop complacency from setting in. Ask yourself, when was the last time you actually did this?

People often think that public speaking should come naturally to me. To the outside world, I seem like a confident, out-going kind of guy. The reality of it is that I can find myself feeling quite shy, particularly when in public situations and under pressure.

I have been best man at my friends' weddings a couple of times, and in 2017, Lee Jones asked me to be his. I had worried about it during the build-up, and when the day arrived, I couldn't think of anything but the speech. The whole wedding passed me by and I can't remember anything of the day, up until the point when it was around half an hour before I was due to give my speech. Many best men reading this will know this feeling. What made it worse, of course, was that everyone was expecting that I would be good at it because I have to talk often and lead the team at Sedulo—but that doesn't involve doing your mate justice on his wedding day and making everyone laugh! Plus, when I am going to do something, I take it very seriously, and I am going to do something to the best of my ability—people will be judging.

Leading up to the speech, anxiety and panic started to set in. My stomach was in knots, my chest tight, and I couldn't remember any of the speech. *Where was it we went again when a certain incident happened?* I was asking myself and looking down at my notes to remember. *Ah, Copenhagen, that's where, of course. That's where it bloody was! I was there in the hotel room at the time being sick all over his bed.* How come I had to look at my written notes to remember where I was, for goodness sake?!

Worry and anxiety had set in, and I was genuinely

thinking of excuses to not go through with it. It passed my mind, given the cold sweats and shortness of breath I was experiencing that I might need to go to hospital anyway and not get to perform my speech after all!

Somehow, I managed to do the talk, and once I was a minute into it, I felt very at home delivering the speech. It seemed to go down well. From that day on, I told myself I would never allow myself to feel like that again, and I would tackle public speaking head-on. I have to admit, reluctantly, that I have done just that, and I started with my old school, by delivering a talk to 500 people at my first public speaking event. I threw myself straight in at the deep end. Subsequently, I have done a little bit of radio, hosted events and of course, launched my own podcast—all of which was scary, unnerving and then…bloody marvellous.

It started to feel good that I was out of my comfort zone and challenging myself, and I realised I had perhaps become stale, repeatedly doing all the things I knew I was good at. I still get edgy, and I don't regard myself as a good public speaker, but I am getting better. More so, I am enjoying the journey it is taking me on.

I urge you to try it. Ask yourself the question—what are you afraid of? How could conquering that fear make you progress? And give it a shot. It worked for me.

Learn to say "no"

You think you're doing everyone a favour by saying "yes" to everything?

"Yes" seems to be easier to say than "no". In truth, by doing this, you are probably spreading yourself too thinly, not placing enough of your focus where it needs to be, and neglecting your own needs at a cost to your own health and well-being.

I got to the age of 40 before I learnt to say "no" emphatically! "No" is better for everyone because it means that when you do say "yes", you really mean it and you are going to do it to the standard you set yourself.

When I learnt to say "no", in business and pleasure, my life became a whole lot better. It created time for me to do the things that mean the most to me. It allowed me to declutter and enjoy doing the activities that improved both my work and my lifestyle, and therefore my work-life balance—regardless of the blurred line—improved substantially.

Are you enjoying the ride?

Whether it's work, lifestyle or a mixture of both, make sure it's fun. Nobody ever reached their deathbed and said they wish they would have had less fun during their time on our planet. Don't confuse this with the belief it should always be fun, either, because that's impossible, and you've got to take the rough with the smooth. But there has to be an underlying enjoyment aspect to what you're doing.

Take action...

1. Mix business with pleasure

Work as hard as you can to make the lines between work and pleasure almost irrelevant.

If you get to this stage, then you must simply love what you do, and how can it be wrong to be consistently doing what you love?

2. Step out of your comfort zone

Challenge yourself, and do things that you wouldn't normally find comfortable. That's how you progress and develop yourself.

Whether this is business or pleasure, it's going to have a positive impact on you as an individual, which will manifest itself in the work or social environment.

Chapter X

Make Sure it's Fun

Shit! I've talked a lot, so far, about the struggles, and I can't apologise for that because that was the motive behind this book, but equally, I can't deny that I have had plenty of fun along the way too.

Don't let life pass you by

I've also talked about living in the moment, primarily within the context of energy and balance, but it's also important that you are enjoying the ride as you go along. It is the ride that brings the most enjoyment, not the destination, as I have illustrated with some examples earlier in this book.

If you would have told me three years ago where my business would be today, I would've replied with sincere conviction that I'd be as happy as anyone could be to achieve what I have. Well, now that I've "arrived" here, am I happy? No. I'm already planning the next stage, visualising what the next phase will look like. What I will also say, though, is that I *have* thoroughly enjoyed the ride. Sometimes I've had to drag myself back into the moment, and it takes practice to truly taste it, because I wasn't fully "living" it. Overall, it's been an awesome journey.

Through Sedulo, I have met many clients who have been struggling and who haven't ever managed to accomplish their business dreams or see their aspirations become a reality. I have also seen clients who have led amazing lives and who continue to do so.

The ones I really feel for aren't the ones who failed to reach their desired destination. It's the ones who struggled and got there, but at their pinnacle forgot to take in that moment—because they had remained so focused on the future—that I feel sorry for. Mentioning no names of course, some of them never appreciated it whilst they had it, and now that they no longer have it, it is their biggest regret.

Enjoy the ride

Becoming successful isn't easy. If it was, everyone would be winning. And they aren't.

We have clients who are consistently achieving their objectives, time after time. There are also others who did well and achieved success but then went and lost it all. Doing well today does not guarantee the same tomorrow.

A client of ours is in the fashion industry. A

few years ago, one of their brands became a household name whilst the company itself was regularly listed as one of *The Times* Fastest-Growing Companies—at least they were before the economic downturn of 2008. That recession put a halt to the company's growth, and since then it's been unable to get close to where it was before the crash. My client's biggest regret? Not enjoying what he had at the time.

Stephen Giblin, a friend who I will mention more about later, had one of the fastest-growing online play-for-fun casinos in the world at one stage, but his success was short-lived—through no fault of his own. Between him and his wife, they built an online business that was so successful, there were over three million downloads of the app and they were attracting 600,000 monthly gamers to their site. For a short while, they earned more than their wildest dreams, but it didn't last forever. His biggest regret? You've guessed it – not living in the moment whilst he had it all.

Steve and Faye are resilient, though, and they bounced back. Now, whilst they may not have reached the same heights as before, they have learnt an important lesson—to appreciate what they have today because it's more than most. Steve is happier now than he ever was before because he is determined, and to re-iterate the point, learning to enjoy the ride as it happens takes practice.

If you're not having fun right now, you need to ask yourself why. If it is temporary, a means to an end, that's fine, but if you're trapped in something that is permanently depriving you of any sense of fun, you need to make changes.

Work hard, play hard

It's fair to say that my journey has been tough and I've had to work hard, but it has also been full of enjoyment.

During the time that the original Sedulo partnership was breaking down, one of our very first clients was enjoying substantial success. Just Search was owned by two brothers, Paul and Justin Yates. The first time I met them, and they won't mind me sharing this, their financial and administrative affairs were in a bit of a state. That said, they were also sat on a brilliant business.

In the early days of what is now called search engine optimisation (SEO), Just Search were one of the UK's leading agencies. Put simply, if you typed "SEO", "SEO agencies", "Search Engine Optimisation" or "Search Engine Optimization" into a Google search, Just Search would be listed among the top three results of the first page, often occupying the top position. And if they could do it for themselves, then they could do it for their clients.

When I met the guys, they had (I think) five members of staff. In those days, Google search wasn't what it is today, basically a virtual high street, and if you wanted to sell screwdrivers and had a better Google-friendly website, you could rank ahead of all the major brands. It was a truly great time for the little guy to be in business.

Nail down the basics

We started by helping Paul and Justin tidy up the financial side of their business, fulfil all their legal obligations and get all their human resource basics in place.

Once we'd got Just Search's legal and financial situation in order, we were able to put together a growth plan with them, which included implementing an almost tenfold increase in their prices—which didn't slow the sales volume—and raising for them a type of bank loan that used to be called a Small Firms Loan Guarantee (SFLG) scheme but is now called an Enterprise Finance Guarantee or EFG loan[5].

These loans are ideal for growing businesses, which tend to be too small to have any assets they can offer as collateral. The bank lends the money because the loan is effectively guaranteed by the UK government.

Accelerate growth

As a result of these activities, the business went from £250k revenue and around £50k losses to £800k revenue and around £300k profit the following year, then to £2.5m revenue and around £800k profit, and finally to £5m revenue and around £2m profit.

The company was growing at what almost seemed like an exponential rate and the clients just got bigger and bigger. We—I say "we" because our partnership with Just Search was so tight—were acting for the likes of Samsung, Regus and Orange, and every month was a record sales month. We had offices in Manchester, but pretty soon we opened in London and Dublin as well.

The whole business was based on having fun on

---

5 An EFG loan is a loan from the bank to a company that has the additional security that the UK government will secure the lender's position.

an almost daily basis. These were plentiful times and money was free-flowing, driven by excellent sales. The brothers would go out and buy a motorbike, drive it outside the office, and it would be gifted to the next person to close a deal! Fun times. Lucrative times.

We worked hard and we played just as hard. It was a great place to be, and it got even better.

They offered me a place on the board, and I snapped their hands off. Sedulo was proving to be such hard work to grow that I often wondered why I was wasting my time with it when I had found this other money spinner, which just continued to make money whilst we travelled the UK partying with our sales teams as reward for the constant flow of record-breaking monthly sales.

Paul approached me and asked me to sell the business on their behalf. I was open and upfront, and I admitted that I'd never sold a business before, but to his credit, and fortunately for me, he said it was me he trusted to do the job and that was that.

Cashing in

I have never been a huge believer in putting a "For Sale" sign on your business if you can sell by other means. It made more sense to attract buyers by marketing how successful we were and making it clear we were most definitely not for sale. Instead, we sponsored awards, sponsored the local professional football team, appeared in all the industry journals, and made sure we had the biggest stands at all the industry exhibitions. This didn't seem like hard work to me!

We soon had three interested parties, and then we received a bid from a Swedish public limited company, which was listed in Sweden at the time, called Getupdated AB.

I still remember the day the bid was put to us as though it was yesterday. We were at a hotel in Cheshire when the bid was verbally offered to us. Paul asked me to join him in the gents restroom, and he could barely contain his emotion. I had only half-opened the door when he jumped on my back and started cheering and jumping up and down. The feeling was one of pure joy. The bid was accepted. Within three years, the business had grown from a start-up to having a sale value of almost £15m—a mixture of up front consideration and further potential bonus earn-outs.

One of the best moments I've experienced in business was being able to tell each of the EMI[6] share option holders, a band of four or five 20-something-year-olds, that each share they owned was now potentially worth £150k.

Play even harder

The brothers were extremely generous after the disposal, and the partying and fun times just got bigger and better. They would think nothing of splashing out tens of thousands of pounds on a night out, ordering expensive bottles of Cristal champagne, and the after-deal party

---

6 An Employee Management Incentive Scheme or EMI is a UK-based scheme which allows employees of a company to be granted share options without giving rise to income tax charges to the employees.

was a perfect example of this.

We spent the weekend in Las Vegas, where we bumped into Mike Tyson. I have mentioned him a few times in this book, so just in case you haven't guessed already, he is one of my boyhood heroes. I can honestly say he was a great bloke to be around—I was totally in awe of him and there are only a few people I'd say that about.

We partied in Hugh Hefner's Los Angeles Playboy Mansion, we hired Ferrari sports cars and Bentleys and drove them through the Nevada desert. Employees flew in private jets, and we paid for all 250 of them to party on board a cruise ship for the weekend. We were in our late twenties and having a ball.

It was a good job we did it while we could, perhaps too extravagantly, because then 2008 arrived…

The whole financial world was about to change.

Take action...

1. Live in the moment

Don't let life pass you by. It's too short, and success can be even shorter.

So enjoy it whilst you have it, embrace the moment as it happens, and appreciate your success along the way. Be careful not to do this at the expense of putting some wool on your back—more on this in the next chapter!

2. Enjoy the ride

Without ups, there are no downs. It doesn't always seem it at the time, but it is the roller coaster of a ride that, in the end, makes it all worthwhile.

The sense of achievement will come once you have ridden the downs—often, the lower the troughs, the more satisfaction is achieved from succeeding.

Chapter XI

Put Some Wool on Your Back

The part I had played in the sale of Just Search, towards the end of 2007, had given me a windfall, but the venture had also given me an intense feeling of untouchability in the business world.

If you've been in a similar situation, it's quite likely that you will recognise that feeling and also likely that things didn't end well. If things are going exceptionally well for you right now, and you are feeling indestructible, this chapter is for you!

Don't invest for the sake of your ego

I'd invested in a bar concept, a women's fashion brand, and a lead generation business, and I had purchased a property in the south of Spain as well as a property within the Mondrian Hotel in South Beach, Miami. Did I have the Midas touch? Definitely not, but I thought I did.

With the benefit of hindsight, I'm grateful social media wasn't around back then! If I am being truthful, I am sure a lot of those investments were driven by ego, despite me attempting to justify it to myself that what I was doing the right thing to do to de-risk my asset portfolio.

If you currently feel as though you are surrounded by the same wall of invincibility, then the chances are you should take note and realign yourself, and make sure you are not making business decisions driven solely by ego. Ego doesn't pay the bills.

In 2008, the global crisis hit and I learnt some big lessons in business.

'Save some wool on your back for a rainy day'

Just before the financial crisis, Just Search had been sold, I'd made my ego-driven investments, and Sedulo had won an award, so we were off to the ceremony for the presentation and to have some more fun.

An older chap, who looked to be in his late sixties, from a company called Ainscough Cranes—a huge business that was far bigger than any of the others I was involved in—was chatting to me. He was asking me how things were going, and I was telling him all about how fantastically well we were doing. As he walked away, he gave me a bit of advice:

'It won't always continue like that, young man. Make sure you save some wool on your back for a rainy day!'

Now, I've already explained that I have great respect for my elders and would usually take on board all the advice that's out there from those who have been there and done it. But on this occasion, I was so full of my own self, I remember thinking *thanks for the advice, mate, but I won't need it.*

It turned out that ignoring his advice was one of the most stupid things I have ever done in business, and I won't make that mistake ever again. Because that rainy day soon came.

I am going to share a story of mine purely to highlight how quickly things can change. It should not only further emphasise how important it is to enjoy the sunshine while it lasts, but should also teach you some lessons about sensibly preparing for the future. I received a harsh lesson on both counts.

Whether my story resonates with you now or at a time further down the line, it may just stop you falling into the same traps that I did.

I constantly live in a sense of fear that this will happen to me again, and I fight myself to grow Sedulo at a rate that takes advantage of opportunity but doesn't put me in the same position I was back then. It's a difficult balance to manage of course.

Be ready for changes in fortune

Things started to go wrong pretty quickly back then, rather than creeping up slowly, so there was no time to react effectively. How I wished I had listened to that gentleman's advice.

For those of you who were not involved in

business in 2008, let me spell out what happened—the global recession hit and the banks put the brakes on most lending, causing worldwide panic and bringing the flow of money almost to a complete halt. Companies in a recession immediately pull back on spending marketing budgets.

My largest client, Getupdated AB, a Swedish stock-listed marketing agency, had only recently acquired Just Search but was now being hit dramatically by the recession as its bank was withdrawing as many of its borrowing facilities as it could from the business. Trade was not good within the business and it was posting losses.

To make matters worse, Sedulo was now owed a lot of money from what was now its most important client.

Any hope I had of being saved by my other investments went out of the window as they were either collapsing or had already failed. The Spanish property lost over 50% of its value and the place in Miami went from having an 80% occupancy rate to below 50%, which meant the income it was generating couldn't cover the mortgage—what had been an asset had changed into a liability almost overnight!

The recession and its repercussions were not the only problems we had to face. It turned out that Just Search wasn't quite the force we had thought it was.

You see, the business was built on front end sales supported by a back end that relied on the fact that we now had access to hundreds of thousands of websites and domains. We could dramatically improve our clients' rankings on Google by linking their sites to the ones we owned, giving them the fuel to power up through Google's rankings. At the time, Google's ranking system was heavily based on backlinks. But Google was about to kick companies like ours right where it hurts.

They updated their algorithm, changing the system they used to rank websites and effectively banning networks such as ours.

And that was it. All our clients tumbled down the rankings within a matter of days. What you have to remember here is that many of our clients had built full online businesses off the back of being able to rank at the top of the search engines for their most relevant search terms, and it was this mechanism that was driving their sales up.

So you can imagine how pissed off they were with us that this method of generating growth had now been removed. The fact that our methods had been instrumental to their success was now irrelevant. Our way of doing things was now the problem, and it was costing them, and me, dearly!

Don't chase profit at the expense of development

It also didn't help that we had cut expenditure on research and development, and customer service, whilst our competitors had been planning and building for the future.

Part of the value of the sale of Just Search in 2007 was based on two earn-out years, 2008 and 2009, so we had made cuts to generate more profit. Now we were paying the price.

Overnight, Just Search—which was the jewel in the crown of Getupdated's portfolio—went from heavy profit making to loss making, at the very time when they most needed the income it had been generating.

Sedulo, heavily reliant upon getting paid from its largest client, no longer had the cash coming in, and the debt was rising steadily.

Things had reached a point where Just Search and Getupdated failing meant that Sedulo was failing.

Don't put all your eggs in one basket

With the global recession and marketing expenditure cuts, Getupdated's bank funding drying up, lack of income from Just Search (and its angry customers to deal with), and my portfolio of investments down the pan, you'd think things couldn't get worse. Wrong.

Unlike other businesses where you can go bust and restart, if you are an accountant and you go bust, it's game over—you lose your licence to practice. Everything was now at stake, the pressure was really on.

Remember the wool? Not only did Sedulo have no wool on its back but neither did I personally. I had invested everything I'd earned from my first major success, the sale of Just Search, and it had all failed.

Fear of failure once more kicked in, and there was only one way out of the situation. I was going to have to help fix both Just Search and its parent company, Getupdated. By turning around their fortunes, Sedulo would start getting paid again, and we'd be saved.

There were multiple problems to fix. Firstly, Just Search was in tax arrears. Secondly, Getupdated had just posted huge losses, so the market capitalisation[7] of the company on the stock market had plummeted to about £8m in total value.

As unfortunate as it was that Sedulo was at risk, so was my reputation, and I had been appointed on the board of Getupdated, which was a publicly listed company as I've explained earlier. Things going wrong with this would have a direct impact on me personally, and that was terrifying.

My life had become a house of cards that was about to collapse at any time, and everything was on the line. It taught me never to put myself in a situation where one card is holding all the others up because if Getupdated had collapsed, it would have truly been game over.

Keep believing in yourself

From 2008 to 2013, my life was nothing but cold sweats, 20-hour days, and hustling—seven days a week. Actually, at Just Search, it would be fairer to say that it sometimes felt as though we were begging—asking clients not to leave, customers to pay, creditors for payment plans, HMRC for leniency, banks to lend us money and people to buy some of our companies.

Every time the phone rang, I would freeze temporarily. Was it a bailiff, a winding up petition, a CCJ, or a supplier cutting us off? Getupdated seemed just one footstep away from failing, and if it did, so

7 Market capitalisation is the value of a company that is traded on the stock market, calculated by multiplying the total number of shares by the present share price.

would Sedulo.

Our invoices to Getupdated were racking up at over £10k per month, and we were owed well over £150k. The problem was that Sedulo's ability to meet its corporation tax bill was totally tied up within that debt, and this tax bill was about to fall due. Within Getupdated, we managed to help the management team change banks, raise funds through two share issues, sell off two subsidiaries, merge with a hosting company, and purchase another hosting company.

In the early days, Getupdated's business model was based on 300 staff working on projects such as website builds and SEO, and cash flow was very much feast or famine. There was no scalability in its product sets, which is why, as it got bigger, it needed more staff and more infrastructure.

A hosting business works in the exact opposite way. People tend not to know who their hosting is with and very few move it around, clients are sticky, and revenue is relatively stable. So with the acquisition of the hosting company, we secured a guaranteed amount of monthly income. We were able to reduce the costs in line with the recurring revenues, and the project-type work became a source of profit. Now we were able to boost this kind of revenue with further hosting acquisitions, allowing us to build from a solid foundation once more.

And so, after almost five years of blood, sweat, tears, absolute pain and my life having been put on hold, we had managed to turn around the fortunes of Getupdated. It had gone from having a market cap of £8m to closer to £60m.

Sedulo got its bill paid, and in turn, paid all its

bills. The situation had been saved.

Learn from your mistakes

The key behind our change in fortune was a Swedish client of mine, and now a friend, Mattias Kaneteg, who is one of the smartest guys I have ever met. Mattias is also a great hustler and extremely intelligent. As the founder of Getupdated and effectively the buyer of Just Search, he was invested in the business for millions—so under just as much pressure to fix things as I was, maybe more so.

Mattias was instrumental in the negotiations to bring inward investment and funding into the business, and he was at the helm when it came to introducing and negotiating the acquisitions of the hosting business, which ultimately saved the group. And saving the Getupdated group probably saved Sedulo in the end.

We still work closely with Mattias on his new project, Miss Group—a global hosting-based business that we have helped him grow through investment and acquisitions globally.

Miss Group is a far cry from the disjointed acquisition structure of the previous project. It is exceptionally focused in what it does and has a rapidly growing profit and valuation. Mattias has learnt from his early career mistakes.

If you can avoid making the mistakes in the first place, great, but sometimes it's unavoidable. Just make sure you don't repeat them, and the key to that is to do things very differently next time. I've listed plenty of my own mistakes and failures throughout this book—

but I have tried to make sure that each one only stood temporarily in the way of succeeding.

I don't think words can do justice to how frightening a period of my business life those times were—I had well and truly learnt my lesson. We'd gone from partying in the Playboy Mansion to begging for survival within a matter of months. Had I listened to my elders (as I usually do!), we would have built the infrastructure to weather a storm. Having allowed myself to get carried away with the money and the feeling of invincibility after the sale of Just Search, I had lost focus on the core business—the day job—and made a whole host of unnecessary investments.

Looking back, I wonder what on earth I was thinking, but we live and learn. It's better to learn by other people's mistakes, so hopefully you can learn a little from mine.

I don't regret what we did, either, because it was a huge learning curve for me and one I was fortunate to learn in my late twenties and early thirties. But I would have done things differently with the benefit of hindsight.

Coming out of the recession, relieved to still be alive in business, I decided to close down every investment that I still had and sell off as much property as I could. I couldn't care less any more about the portrayal of my success to others, and if you haven't learnt this yet, then I suggest you take it on board.

You must try and build your business on fundamentally strong foundations—analysing risks and constantly mitigating them. Try to avoid investing in bullshit ideas because they appear glamorous, and make sure you focus on your core business until it has reached its full potential.

I had been through plenty of ups and downs, and it had been a thrilling ride, but I learnt my lesson and realised back then that I didn't want to continue like that. I promised myself that my focus would be on strengthening the foundations of Sedulo and painstakingly building up each area of that business, brick by brick.

Take action...

1. Put some wool on your back

Even if you have a successful business, with a good track record, you may still face adversity in times of trouble. Sometimes it's through no fault of your own, such as an economic crash.

As soon as you are able, create a financial cushion to soften the blow, should something unexpected happen. This should allow you to dust yourself off and keep going.

2. Learn from your mistakes

Accept you are going to make plenty of mistakes in business. Use them as your guide to the future.

The people who ultimately fail are the people who make those same mistakes over and over again. With every mistake comes a lesson—learn from it.

Chapter XII

Grow Your Culture

I can't overstate the importance of remaining focused on one core project. Mine was back on the main company I owned, Sedulo. I had a plan in my head, a blueprint for growing the business, so I set about working towards that goal.

I really believe you are only ever going to be as good as the people you have around you on the journey, so I set about developing a culture and a winning team—that was the cornerstone of what I wanted to build, and if you're employing staff, it should be yours too.

Sedulo's culture is its main asset, one that I don't see in a lot of other businesses, including those in far sexier industries than mine, and I don't get why.

Building a culture organically

If you're in the early years of your company's growth, you will find it much easier to create the team's culture, because change is one of the hardest things to push through a business. Start with your cultural values and a determination to align your culture to these as early as possible.

There are many other people in professional advisory firms who want to have a variation of what Sedulo has created today, but they can't get the whole organisation to want to adapt. The common excuse is "we are too big, now, to do what you guys are doing", and I see that obstacle to them as being a real opportunity to us. The sooner you do it, the better!

When you have fewer employees, it is much easier to get your team to adopt your values. You can speak directly with each one of them. It's likely that your first few team members will be a good reflection of what you like in people, and hopefully they will feel the same about you—so the buy-in will be at its strongest point.

Define your values

It's important to decide the values of the business as soon as possible and to share your vision with your team, clearly communicating what it means to them. They need to know what this looks like in terms of the behaviours attached to them.

Make sure you're measuring your attempt to create them. At Sedulo, we assess each member of staff every six months and score them on how closely they are representing our values. This score is taken into consideration as part of their annual appraisal and pay review, so how people are rewarded is based on these principles.

But expectations cut both ways, so we also get the staff to score the company on those same values every six months as part of a staff-satisfaction survey—or "happiness survey" as we now call it.

When you come up with your company's values, make sure they come from you if you're the owner, or a mixture of you and your close management team. I don't get the idea of hiring in third parties to create your culture. That's artificial and lacking in authenticity—besides, the company is a representation of you, so who knows how you want your business to be more than you do? So save yourself some money and define your company's values yourself.

I didn't have to spend too long thinking about Sedulo's because they came naturally—they were everything I *couldn't* see being offered in our marketplace at the time. These core values are still at the heart of everything we do, even now that we have grown to over 100 advisors.

Compared to some businesses that pay lip service to their core values, I think sometimes our new recruits are taken aback at how real ours are to me. I really do fucking mean them!

We have six values and they are simple:

1 Entrepreneurial—make your clients make more money

2. Personable—deliver your advice with character
3. Hands-on—know your client, for goodness' sake
4. Offer value for money—when you send your bill, make sure the client is delighted to pay it
5. Holistic—give the client the multi-disciplined financial advice they need
6. Community— give back

We have three HR pillars, which we also live by as a company:

1. Get results, together
2. Have fun, together
3. Give back, together

What's in it for them?

We are often guilty of thinking as business owners when we need to think more from an employee perspective. How would you feel if you went into work every day without being given a clear and concise direction? And this is a big problem with business owners like you and me. We create a set of values, we talk about the direction of the business, and we produce mission statements, but we don't tell the employee what's in it for them.

What is in it for them? Let's be honest, here. As much as you are friends with some of them in the early days, your relationship with them is going to change as the business grows, and anyway, your team will not care half as much about your targets and milestones if they can't see what it means to them and how they will personally benefit—and why should they?

There's an old joke about an employee and his boss:

The boss arrived at work in a brand new Lamborghini. His employee stood there, admiring his boss's new car. 'Wow," he said. 'That's an amazing car!' His boss smiled and said, 'If you work hard, put all your hours in and strive for excellence, I'll be able to get another one next year!'

Whilst this does make me chuckle, it also carries a great message about how you might be perceived. Make sure you develop and pay people as a reflection of their performance and in line with achievement of your company values, and you will have a highly motivated and highly aligned team.

Value your team

Whilst pay is a motivator in the workplace, it is not the only ingredient for building a highly motivated workforce.

At Sedulo, we've always taken our staff away on holiday for the Christmas parties. Our very first party was in Dublin, although from memory it was just me and Lee!

Since then, we have been to Majorca, Milan, Barcelona, Lagos, and just recently, we took most of our team to Estepona, in Spain.

After the first two years in the office that had looked like a brothel, where we had stayed to complete our lease from Sedulo version 1.0, we moved to a great space on the canal in the centre of Manchester. It was important, even in the early days, to provide the best working environment that we could afford.

We'd always had fresh fruit delivered, a minibar stocked with non-alcoholic and alcoholic beverages for people who wanted to stay late after work and have a beer or glass of wine, and we had social events going on constantly.

In the summer, people were free to move outside, sit next to the canal, and work in the sunshine.
More recently, we have introduced a well-being process, whereby experts have been coming in to teach such things as how to handle stress, meditation, breathing techniques, and nutrition.

I have always been an advocate of preparing for performance, and I am a firm believer that if you want to be at the top of your sport, you have to work all week on the preparation. A Premier League footballer's life revolves around preparing for the game. They don't eat a Chinese meal the night before, or indulge in late-night drinking, and then expect to deliver peak performance. I don't see the difference between the athlete's performance and an employee's performance—for either of them to perform at their best, they need to prepare correctly. At Sedulo, we try to educate our team on how to best prepare for what they do.

Sir Richard Branson explained it perfectly with these words:

'Clients do not come first. Employees come first. If you take care of your employees, they will take care of the clients.'

I couldn't agree more.

Now don't get me wrong—we did everything

we could to cultivate a relaxed environment, designed to allow our team to work at an optimal level, but our work is far from relaxing. We have a client base of businesses that are growing furiously in some cases, and they expect us to be around when they want us. Whether you're talking weekends, late evenings or the crack of dawn, we are there for them. The work at Sedulo always has been, and still is, a high-pressure environment.

The business world has shifted its focus, once more, towards creating the right environment for staff to work in. I say 'once more' because whilst we tend to think of the modern world as far more advanced than the 19th century, a quick visit to the factory of world-famous confectioner Cadbury, in Birmingham, reveals that what they were doing in the 1800s was well ahead of its time in terms of funky workspaces, even by today's standards.

Cadbury was one of the first companies to introduce half-day working on Saturdays, and one of the first to build houses, parks, sports pitches and gymnasiums for its employees.

As a sign of our respect for Cadbury, as a pioneer in creating staff happiness, we've designed one of our boardrooms in Leeds around the theme of the company and its founder, John Cadbury. And chocolate is freely available all day, every day, for staff and clients!

Maintaining the culture

As your business grows and the number of staff you employ starts to rise, you are going to encounter tangible milestones that will each present their own challenges. I've identified four stages of growth that I have experienced for myself whilst building Sedulo, and I am going to highlight some of the cultural differences that I've experienced between each stage.

The beginning—0 to 10 staff

As I said earlier, this is possibly the easiest stage for creating your culture. You will know everyone personally, and in the main, you can expect everyone to be heading in the same direction. If there are any members of your team not connecting with your plan and values at this stage, just cut them off—because it will get harder from here.

During our earliest stage of growth, we had a core of seven lads, who were all in their twenties, and my mum who held it all together. We would work hard together and play hard together.

Most of the people we had working for us during the early days were cut from the same cloth, and there were real benefits from this at the start. But as we grew to around 7–8 staff, I started to see that having a team with such similar characteristics had as many negatives as it did positives.

Everyone was becoming a clone, so whilst what the whole team did overall was good, anything that was done poorly also tended to be replicated across the team. The team was male dominated, and it didn't feel as though we had a balanced approach to problem solving or a mixture of solutions. I made sure the next few recruits were female members, with more balanced personalities, and I added in some more experienced staff.

In the very early stage of our development, to create a culture, I needed bodies. I was very focused on growing the team rather than focusing on profits, because I felt that having more bums on seats created a better atmosphere and structure for the future.

Whilst we didn't have much money in those days, it created an opportunity for us to bring in apprentices on a lower wage and give them training and a route to becoming an accountant. It also gave us a pipeline of staff members further down the line who had been bought into Sedulo from a very early age, and some of these early trainees are crucial to our business today.

It took us about three years to get to 10 staff, with revenue of about £500k—so around £50k per annum of revenue per employee, a metric we have constantly measured against our industry average. We knew at the time that £50k of revenue per member of staff was low by industry standards, but in a growing business you can't expect to hit the metrics of an established business. We have worked to improve this over time.

A growing team—10 to 20 staff

Once your team's size exceeds 10 people, if you're doing things in the same way you did before, you're heading for your next big problem—because at this stage, you should start to realise that for a team to work, you need an even greater and more diverse range of skill sets and personalities.

You still probably know everyone on a personal basis, and the belief in the core values that holds you and the management team together will remain strong.

Issues arise with the wider team. I realised quickly that the "lad culture" that had brought us to £500k turnover was starting to hold Sedulo back.

By the time we had 20 staff, we had a male to female ratio of 50:50 and an array of age and experience within the team—our culture had to adapt. On a separate note, bringing in age and experience drives up the costs. Nevertheless, it is necessary.

We went from 10 staff to 20 staff in about the same amount of time as it had taken us to grow to the first 10—about three years—and brought in a further £500k of revenue. At this point, we had 20 staff and £1m of revenue, again sticking close to the £50k per employee per annum metric.

I have heard some of our larger clients suggest that their favourite size of team was when they had around 20 staff. At this point, you can still have a one-to-one with each of them, but you also really feel as though you have a proper business. I did enjoy this stage too, but I have to be honest and add that so far, as we have become even bigger, so too have the challenges, and overcoming these has been even more rewarding.

A larger team—20 to 50 staff

Once we had a few more than 20 staff—maybe 23 or so—it seemed as though something had drastically changed. I didn't know so much about the last three hires personally, and it just felt as though we had gone from 20 to 50 staff, not to 23.

These new staff members started arriving at 9am and putting their coats on at 5:30pm—it all felt alien to me! All of a sudden, I was being told our processes weren't working. It felt as though we had lost some control just because of the addition of just two or three staff members, I couldn't explain it then and I can't now!

The wheels started falling off, the structure couldn't handle it, and the internal HR person—probably the office manager for your business but my mum in our case—was starting to feel uneasy. Wages were now £75k a month or nearly £1m a year! *How the fuck did that happen?* It was all starting to get real...staff appraisals in the pub after work were a thing of the past from here on in!

If your business is within this size bracket right now, you will get exactly what I am saying. Don't overthink it because you won't find all the answers. Keep adapting processes and systems and push through, because it gets slightly easier again—for a short while.

Growing from 20 to 30 staff seemed like a huge jump for us, but that's where the pain was—growing from 30 to 50 was far easier.

We went from having a team of 20 to 45 during the two-year period of 2015–2017.

Much larger—50 to 100 staff

You made it to 50 staff?

Oh my God, you're thinking. *I thought we had control of this! I thought we had put these systems in place at 20 staff—why have they stopped working? Whose fault is this?* you're asking yourself, looking to the HR manager to blame. Except for the fact that—err—you don't have a HR manager, or a finance person, and your staff are fed up with the outsourced IT solution that put you in a ticketing system.

Your world is falling apart at the 50-staff mark... *Fuck! Why now, when we've only just started to make some bloody profit?* Sorry guys, but at this point, you're going to have to spend that profit on bringing in your centralised function, because if you don't invest in that foundation now, you're going to have a collapsing empire as you move beyond 50 staff.

You are now relying on a management team to instil your culture. *What management team?* you're asking.

That's right, the team comprising those who remain from your first 10 recruits.

That one that consists of people who have never managed anyone ever before, people who have been on no training courses, and people who do not have the experience to do what they are being asked to do.

That management team—the one that's full of your mates if you were anything like me with Sedulo, and full of people who are all great at *doing their jobs.*

And they are concentrating so hard on the additional task of management that they have never done before, that they forget…

The culture—the bloody CULTURE!

So you have to start again, instilling your culture and values back into the team.

Now my team has not grown to much greater than 100 staff, but I have heard from many people that getting to this point is the toughest part of building a business.

When I spoke to JD Sports chairman, Peter

Cowgill, who employs over 30,000 people, he explained that he has various management teams, so he has direct contact with many fewer than 100 of his organisation's employees.

Andrew Mason, the CEO of Groupon, showed a similar perspective in an interview: 'Well, the hardest part is actually kind of 20 to 100. I'd say that's the most disorientating part.' This is his perspective, despite the fact that Groupon went on to employ thousands of staff beyond that point, of course.

So, if you've grown your business to over 100 staff, the chances are that you're pretty successful and you've mastered the staff culture anyway.

At Sedulo, we grew from 50 to almost 100 staff during our eighth year, with a large chunk of that growth coming from an acquisition, and that took us to being one of the largest 1% of accountancy firms in the UK.

Managing culture within an acquisition scenario

It's tough enough to keep control of your culture whilst you're growing organically—it's another thing altogether when you've acquired somebody else's and have to change it to yours.

Early 2018, Sedulo acquired Bartfields, a traditional compliance accountancy firm based near the centre of Leeds.

Bartfields was founded in 1927 by brothers Isaac and Sam Bartfield. By the time we acquired it, the firm employed 35 people who were mostly in their late fifties, and five of their staff members had served the firm for over 40 years!

They were based in Headingley, around five miles from Leeds city centre, in the kind of office that was typical of an old-school firm—visitors were greeted with brown desks, ceiling tiles, blue carpet tiles and what looked like the world's biggest stockpile of accountancy books and records! It's plain to see that Bartfield's culture was a million miles from ours.

Each acquisition situation is different so there is no one piece of advice I can give you that is going to work for every individual acquisition, but I can tell you about my experience and highlight the parts that may benefit you.

Respect the legacy of others

Throughout this book, I've mentioned how important it is to respect your elders, and that became an essential consideration now that I had become the new owner of a company with a 91-year history! My thoughts immediately turned to figuring out how to pay tribute to this firm's notable heritage in the same way that I'd hope whoever owns Sedulo in another 100 years from now will pay respect to me.

Fortunately for me, a previous employee—who'd worked at Bartfields for four decades since starting with the firm at its inception in the 1940s—had written their memoirs as they were leaving the business in the 1980s. Those notes told me everything I needed to know to be able to pay full respect to the firm's history.

When companies are acquired, I have seen situations where the new owners have taken immediate steps to remove all reminders of the past and imprint their own values. One business owner told me the first thing they did, having acquired another company, was to throw the founder's desk into a nearby skip. I have seen this methodology work for others but it's not for me. We wanted both staff and clients to stay—if we wanted the clients to remain with us, we needed to make sure the staff wanted to as well.

We started by introducing the same perks that we already provide in our Manchester office, which includes morning breakfast, afternoon tea, massage etc., and we carried out a staff-satisfaction survey to get a base score of the level of happiness throughout the team, in line with our core values. This was immediately followed up with appraisals, and every member of staff was given their own personal development plan, again linked to our core values.

The whole Bartfield team was going to be moved to a new location in the centre of Leeds. We chose St Paul's House, a beautiful 19th century building situated in Park Square, and the new office is based on the ground floor, which overlooks the park. To make the transition as smooth as possible for the Bartfield staff, we announced the move two months in advance and made sure nobody was out of pocket, reimbursing them for expenses such as extra travel costs.

During the TUPE[8] consultation concerning the transfer of staff to Sedulo, I gave in on almost everything, not because I am weak—far from it—but because if I was

---

8 TUPE refers to the transfer of undertakings (protection of employment) regulations 2006. These rules protect employees' rights when the organisation transfers to a new employer.

going to make this work, I needed my newly acquired team to buy into everything we were trying to achieve.

Blend the old with the new

Remember, I wanted to pay tribute to Bartfield's significant heritage, so we designed the new office fit-out to blend the old with the new. Sedulo's Leeds office has a really modern feel to it but also captures Bartfield's original brand and history perfectly.

One of the first things you will notice when you walk into the reception area of the Leeds office, is a quote that goes all the way back to when Bartfields was founded in 1927. It is written in large letters on the wall behind the reception desk:

'Tell me, Dorothy—I'm marvellous, I'm brilliant, I'm good looking, I'm charming.'

According to the memoirs I managed to obtain, these are the words that Isaac's personal assistant, Dorothy, had to welcome him with on a daily basis. Now everyone who enters our Leeds office is greeted with those same words almost 100 years on.

The quote was verified, around four weeks after we had opened, when a lady came into the office and asked me, with a voice filled with emotion, why we had her great grandfather's favourite quote on our wall. She'd been taking lunch in the park, and the large words had caught her eye by chance. It was clear that she was touched by the fact that we had paid such respect to her great grandfather, and it was a lovely conversation to have.

The reception area has been designed with a

1920s Great Gatsby bar theme in mind, and one of the boardrooms is named The Bartfields suite. All the old shareholder agreements and accounts have been framed and wall-mounted along with a framed list of previous partners. I thought it would be a nice touch to pay respects to the employees that lost their lives during the Second World War, and also to a previous trainee-turned-partner who'd sadly lost his life in a tragic car accident in the 1980s.

I learnt that the partners of the firm had held a tennis tournament in the 1970s, so we built an indoor Wimbledon-style garden complete with a table tennis court. We named this the Fred Perry suite because I am from the same place as Fred—Stockport!

Finally, as well as inviting the usual press and the city's movers and shakers to our launch night, we also invited all the former partners of Bartfields, along with the family of the firm's original founders. It was a great night, and there were plenty of smiles and tears as people reflected on what we had done.

As I write this book, we are just at the end of the first year post acquisition, we have retained almost all of the clients and lost only four of the original 40 staff members we inherited from Bartfields—a figure that would be natural churn in any business anyway.

One of the surprises that we encountered came with how readily the older generation, many of whom were close to retirement, took to Sedulo and its modern culture. We'd thought we could compensate for any potential lack of enthusiasm from the older heads by developing the younger members of the team, who we expected to embrace the Sedulo way of doing things.

Well, we couldn't have been more mistaken.

Some of the more experienced members absolutely loved what we did, volunteering to help with the move, getting involved with our events and generally getting stuck in. By contrast, three of the four people who left us were in their twenties—being a part of one of the fastest-growing accounting firms in the UK was simply too much for them, it seemed!

Be authentic

We have built a culture in Sedulo by being authentic, and everything we do is for a reason, because that's what we believe in. I will mention this authenticity throughout the book. There are so many times when I think businesses do things with an ulterior motive, but in the end I believe this manufactured strategy gets found out and fails to create the expected result. We don't put a sweet shop in our office because we think it's a good gimmick. We do it because we truly *want* our team to love coming to work and enjoy their working environment as much as they possibly can.

I am hoping Mr Cowgill and Mr Mason are both right about their staff numbers, because we have grown our team to over 100 staff and I am hoping the toughest part has been done.

You cannot do everything on your own, and growing the culture is just as necessary as putting together a winning team.

Take action...

1. Create a set of values

To create a company that you want, you need a team to help you achieve it. Have clear, defined values that represent everything you want your business to be known for. And make them genuine, honest and authentic. That way, your passion and drive to see these develop within your company is going to be stronger.

2. Let the team know what's in it for them

Make sure your team know what the defined values are, measure their performance against them, and make sure they are rewarded for emulating them.

Chapter XIII

Create a Winning Team

No matter whose story you've read, they will have teamed up with someone, or a bunch of people, to have made things happen. If you haven't learnt this rule yet, it's best you drop whatever else you're doing now and learn it fast—you shouldn't be the most talented person in your team. Even more importantly, every member of your management team needs to know this.

How not to create a winning team

There are several simple mistakes that I see regularly across many of the companies that I advise, and you need to avoid them.

Not owning your sales

Make sure the first people you employ into your business are not responsible for the sales. This is one of the most common mistakes that I come across. In a brand-new business, usually *the* most important task is to bring in sales. Why would you trust someone else to do *the* most important task? Plus, sales people are expensive.

So I think you need to give serious consideration to taking it upon yourself to be the one who owns the responsibility of bringing in *your* sales. You can then build a team around your sales.

In Sedulo, I was the sales guy, and my first recruits were:

- Lee, my right-hand man and an amazing accountant
- Mum, to run all administration, operations, and to keep us in check
- Dan Wilson, who was a trainee graduate at the time (now a partner of the firm!), and someone who could give me a high level of intelligence at a price I was able to afford back then

Bringing in clients rested with me! Even today, I probably bring in more direct sales than anyone else in the company.

Promoting out of loyalty

Another don't. Don't hire or promote people to be managers out of loyalty or because they are good at their job. Why? Because someone being good at their job won't necessarily mean they possess the skills required for management.

I'm going to be candid here and say this *is* a mistake that we made in Sedulo, but what I have realised since, and have to admit, is this: when this happens, it's not their fault, and it's not fair on them. It's yours, and it's also going to be damaging to both them and you as you move forward. You must be honest with people here and do the right thing. People must be in the jobs that are best suited for their skill sets, and if they're not, change the situation.

Recruiting poor talent

I have never had an issue with recruiting people who can do things better than me, and you should be the same. And you should make sure your management team follows suit.

Managers, or more accurately, poor managers, tend to want to recruit people who are worse than themselves. Why? Because they want to protect their position. It doesn't make them bad people—it makes them human—but their failure to employ the best staff they can find will prove detrimental to your business in the long run. If you look around your business right now, I can bet you can find evidence of this. If you can't, fantastic. If you can, then you need to nip it in the bud immediately because if you don't, it will be obstructive to the progression of your business. This is another mistake that I allowed to happen in the earlier years at Sedulo and had to correct later.

Neglecting leadership

Recruiting a management team is hard enough, but what you really need in your organisation are leaders. Motivation and inspiration come from leaders, not management. I take this role very seriously, although I have far from mastered it.

I love, and try to put into action, this statement from Thomas J. Peters, an American writer on business management: 'Leaders don't create followers. They create more leaders.'

Understanding your company values is critical to your business. But understanding them is not enough. It is essential that you live up to them.

If you look at Manchester United's most successful manager, Sir Alex Ferguson, you will see a fine example of how to consistently lead a team. He created a core set of values for the club and didn't allow any deviation from them. If rules were broken, the offender was out, regardless of their position within the club—nobody was indispensable—and he was able to do this because he upheld the rules and values himself.

On the other side of the city, the current Manchester City boss, Pep Guardiola, is achieving similar success. He believes in a particular way of behaving and playing, and his team lives and breathes his vision in everything they do. You can see Pep's principles in action in the way the team performs. His players don't panic when things aren't going according to plan, just as their leader kept a cool head during the 2016/17 season when his methods were being called into question due to a lack of immediate success. He stayed true to his values and Manchester City went on to win the Premier League at the end of a record-breaking season in 2017/2018.

I have always preferred being a leader to being a manager anyway, but it requires constant self-development.

How to build a winning team

Now that you know about some of the more common mistakes, let me share some tips with you to help you build a stronger team.

Get a wing-person

I have spoken already about how lonely a place it can be at the top of an organisation. When I first set up Sedulo with my former business partner who I mentioned earlier, the first person we ever hired was a guy called Lee Jones, and he's been alongside me ever since. Lee came with me after the split from my business partner, when I took full control of Sedulo. He has continued to be an asset to the firm and someone I can count on in critical situations. Now he is also an owner of the business.

When it comes to your right-hand person, your wing-person, the most important things are to know you can trust them, 100%, and that they believe, 100%, in what you are trying to achieve with the vision you have set. You must have a wing-person you can completely rely upon. For me, it's Lee.

We disagree on plenty, and that's good because if my first recruit had been too much like me, Sedulo would have been wiped out within the first three years—

which is what happens to a large proportion of other businesses.

Find a partner that complements you rather than replicates you. Lee is good at the things I am not. For a start, I like to talk but he likes to do. I like to look at the future strategy. He likes to scrutinise the details, identify potential problems and figure out ways to deal with them.

Choose your adviser wisely

If you can't get that person internally, find one temporarily through an external channel. I am not here to sell you my services, but I have made a living out of being a sounding board, and Sedulo has grown out of exactly that—it's not fun to be lonely.

It sometimes staggers me how long people stay with an accountant who they have to chase to speak to once a year. A decent accountant should be your friend. If you're feeling as though you're on your own, your accountant is failing you—change them immediately, and find one that cares about you. Do it now.

Embrace diverse characters

As I mentioned in the last chapter on culture, you need a diverse range of personalities in your business and management team. You've already been introduced to Lee. Now I am going to tell you about our other shareholders. They are all quite different, and all add value in their own unique ways.

Benn Longshaw is our corporate finance partner.

Whilst he is generally quite an introverted and quiet personality, he is an extremely credible and reliable individual. Benn was brought on board relatively early in our firm's history, purposely because of his laid-back approach and his integrity.

He was exactly what Lee and I needed, providing balance, and perfectly complementing our extrovert and 100mph approach to things.

So was Dan Wilson, our audit partner. With a personality that is much closer to Benn's, he is another great foil for me and Lee. As Dan is still relatively young, he has an experienced mentor, Joanne, who is helping him develop his technical skill set.

Our tax partner, David Evans, is another of the same ilk as Benn and Dan, and he is also one of the younger members of the management team. His mentor, Darrell, has run tax teams for almost 30 years!

Leyton Jeffs is our funding partner. His banking team sources and completes on over 300 deals a year, and you don't do that if you're quiet, shy and introverted. He is cut from the same cloth as me and Lee. Remember what I said about employing people who are better than you? Leyton provides the competition that I need to keep me on my toes and question what I am delivering in terms of value to the business. Staying hungry, keen and competitive is very important in a growing and maturing business, and working with great people maintains this.

Cathryn Wright is our group MD, having previously been managing director of LGBT charity Stonewall. Cathryn has the ability to see things from a completely different perspective than all of us, and we have become much more of a progressive business since her appointment in 2018. She is the gel that bonds the rest of us together, which makes us operate even more effectively. Cathryn works closely with Max Draper, who was her CFO at Stonewall, and the two of them now run our London office, whilst Max is now also our group CFO.

The team works well because its collective value is greater than the sum of the individual parts, and you should look for this when building your own winning team.

Make sure you incentivise in the right way

The ownership structure is important. It can play a pivotal role in how your company performs, and it is paramount for ensuring Sedulo's ongoing success. It's important you get this structure right as early as you can in your journey.

Within the professional services industry, it is normal for partners to buy in to the partnership. They gain access to profits for as long as they are partners. Then, when they retire, they get their "buy-in money" back, but this incentivises stakeholders to focus on short-term profit. Why should they care about the long-term growth of the company, 20–30 years down the line, when there is no gain for them?

Sedulo's structure is the opposite of the structure of most of our competitors, and this is a major contributor to our success.

We are a group of eight limited companies, and when someone buys in to become a partner at Sedulo, they get a shareholding in either the group or their specific subsidiary. They do so with the knowledge that the equity value of their stake will increase as we grow—so when they sell, they will benefit from the additional value created throughout their ownership, and that provides the incentive to think about the future growth of the firm.

At Sedulo, we focus on the long term, as a business and also in terms of how we serve our clients. There is no need for us to make money from our clients quickly, so we can share the journey with them and create the most value for us when we've created the most value for them—on exit.

Our ownership structure matches and facilitates our vision of growth. This structure is a fundamental reason why we have enjoyed as much success as we have, and also one of the reasons why traditional firms will struggle to adopt the same long-term approach to business and clients that has worked for us. It will be very difficult for them to change. And so we maintain an advantage over our competitors as a result.

Now you know how I built a management structure, but you need to look beyond that and look to the future. Ask yourself where the next batch of management material and leaders are coming from.

When I asked myself that same question in Sedulo, I realised we weren't developing the next generation of leaders. So we started a progression structure that has created a fast-track path for staff to advance and will ensure our senior management team going forward.

Our Sedulo Accelerator Scheme (SAS) was developed for the younger generation of talent in our team, who we believe will go on to become senior managers within the next 5–10 years. The scheme was built with diversity in mind, to make sure the next batch of management recruits reflects how we see the progression of the firm in the future. People within the scheme get access to internal and external mentoring as well as additional coaching and leadership days to expedite the pace of their development.

Build an external team

Having an external support mechanism is just as important as an internal one, and I have made a living out of providing this solution to people who need it. Your external team should also give you a foundation to keep learning and developing yourself, and as I said earlier, to be a leader you have to keep evolving yourself.

I recently had the privilege of interviewing Andy Grant, who has an amazing story. Andy is an ex-marine who was unfortunately blown up serving his country in Afghanistan. He decided to take the decision to amputate one of his legs, and since then, has won gold at the Invictus Games, broke the world record for running the 10km in a time of 37 minutes and written a book, amongst a whole host of other achievements.

One of the key reasons for his success, he explained, is that he surrounds himself with people who are already in the world in which he wants to succeed. He gave me a piece of advice: 'if you're the smartest person in the room, Paul, you need to change rooms!' This is something that has stuck with me since, and I have constantly tried to surround myself with people who can help me grow.

Getting external advice on your business often leads to the best ideas. People within the business are often constrained by their knowledge of how things are already done in the business. When you have a problem, you don't always want ideas that are similar to what you already do, because that's caused the problem in the first place! Thinking outside of the box is difficult if you're constantly living *in* the box.

I am in the process of creating an advisory board at Sedulo to advise me on how to progress the company. There won't be any accountants or tax advisors on this! It will be a board of entrepreneurs that think entrepreneurially.

For example, I've included Gary Palmer, who is originally from California—a larger-than-life character who is a director of the car hire company, Enterprise Cars. Gary doesn't give me advice on how an accountancy firm should be run. He gives me advice on how a forward-thinking business should operate.

I am fortunate that I get to hang out with my clients, some of whom are very successful, so I have an open book of business contacts. I am a member of a chief executive's club where we meet once a month, too, and that was where I got introduced to Nikki Owen who subsequently got me into the meditation I mentioned earlier.

So I have this external network that I have created, but most importantly to me, I also have my family—and a guy called Steve who I will tell you about, shortly. But first...

Aim for a balanced family life

I know what it is like to run businesses as a young, single person, and as a married family man, and I can tell you it's easier to run your business when you are living in a settled environment. I can also tell you, in the main, that people who are more successful tend to focus on maintaining a settled home life, and balancing this with social activities such as going out and partying requires a conscious effort. For me, becoming successful is about living the life as much as it is about what you do in your working hours.

As I mentioned earlier, I am married to Zeri and we have three young boys together, but achieving a relatively stress-free home life wasn't easy.

Zeri has her own business, and she has done a reasonable amount of acting over the years. For almost two years, from being almost newborn, our youngest son, Romeo, was also an actor and recently played the part of George Appleton in the ITV soap *Coronation Street*. That took up a lot of Zeri's time, but her main focus is the running of the house. I have learnt to let her run that domain, but I can tell you that letting go and leaving her to it didn't come naturally to me, and it's probably the same for you, because as business owners we like to be in control, right?

Read on and this might just save your relationship!

I used to come home from work, put down my laptop, and immediately make for the kids. Then I would play with them, and get them all excited and jovial—just as they were about to go to bed, which was around half an hour after Zeri, bless her, had got them into their pyjamas, given them their supper and calmed them down, ready to sleep. I used to think she was wrong for stopping me from playing with them because I hadn't seen them all day...

Until I watched a programme, featuring Theo Paphitis from BBC's *Dragons' Den*, where he was saying that he pretty much left control of the household to his wife. I took this on board. It wasn't easy and took a fair amount of practice on my behalf, but now Zeri runs every aspect of the home environment. She's in charge of the house, and why shouldn't she be? She's the one who spends all day there whilst I am at my work. Now I come home to an atmosphere of peace and tranquillity, and that's especially important to someone like me.

Giving up control of the house—of anything—took a while to get used to, but having clearly defined boundaries has helped. Zeri is a vital part of my overall team, and she is also an essential sounding board for me, allowing me to vent on an almost daily basis and giving me back my self-belief when self-doubt starts to kick in.

Our three boys play a huge part in bringing me into the present moment—which is essential, as I mentioned earlier, for balancing my mental health. Given that I had early-stage disruption in my family as a child, spending time with Zeri and the boys, being a family, is very important to me.

Find your Steve

When looking for a sound board, sometimes business owners concentrate on finding people who have the right qualifications or previous experience. I am not saying these people aren't helpful, but I have a different solution.

One of the most valuable people in my life is my good friend Steve Giblin. Now Steve is in his fifties and is a successful guy in his own right, but he doesn't think so because in his mind he's just a working-class lad from Hulme, Manchester, who speaks with a broad accent and gets most of his words mixed up. But the fact is that he owns a play-for-fun online game called Gambino Poker, which was once one of the largest poker sites in the world, generating more than three million downloads within a matter of months.

For a short time, at least, Steve achieved success beyond his wildest dreams, but then, for whatever reason, he lost control of his game, trusted others with it more than he trusted himself, and the whole thing collapsed. This left him and his wife, Faye, in a lot of financial trouble and they almost lost everything.

But just three years later, Faye and Steve managed to pick themselves up off the floor, launch another couple of businesses and regain control of Gambino. If they ever write a book, I urge you to read it, because to have shown such determination, resilience and persistence, and to have achieved what they have, is a phenomenal achievement.

One day, I got talking to Steve about Gambino, and one phone call led to another until it evolved into a daily phone call, and it's been a daily phone call for almost six years now. We chat for half an hour every morning while I am driving to work and he is walking his dog. It would be nice to think it is a two-way conversation, but

I suspect it is mainly me pouring out what happened the day before and listing all the things I am going to tackle head-on that day.

It takes a special person to sit and listen, and he has been there for me as I have discussed the ups and downs of my business life. Steve is one of those people who genuinely wants others to be as successful as they can be. When he went through his own crisis, even during the toughest times when he was struggling to make ends meet, he still wanted to listen to how much my business was growing and how successful we were becoming.

Steve has been an absolute blessing to me. He is much wiser than he realises, and he's provided me with some great advice over the years, but mostly he has been there when I've wanted to blow off steam or blow my own trumpet. The fact that he isn't in my business, and he doesn't have the constraints of running a business like mine, has also helped.

I have talked a lot in this chapter about some of the people around me, and I have done this purposely to highlight the array of people that are in the winning team I have put together. You can see that there is a mix of internal and external members and they all have a role to play.

If you haven't already, get working on creating your team, because you aren't going to achieve too much without it.

Take action...

1. Build a diverse team

It is likely that your customers or clients are going to be diverse, and you need an internal team that understands your customers in order to sell more products and services. Therefore, you need a diverse team.

2. Have an external team

It is lonely being a business owner. We have established that.

You need to build a support mechanism outside of the working environment that gives you fresh thinking and unbiased, no strings attached advice on your business.

Chapter XIV

Lay Solid Foundations

The staff and culture are the bedrock of any business, and it took me a long time to get these to where I wanted them within Sedulo. It's a movable feast and something I am constantly adding to and tweaking. Once you have it in place, you need to look at other foundations you need to lay within your business. I come across lots of businesses where they have just not created solid infrastructure on which to build.

Grow with solid revenues

I can't reiterate enough how much you should try to focus on coming up with ways to create recurring revenues for your business. I don't mean thinking about the situation in the way you always have done—where new lines of recurring revenue currently don't exist. I mean thinking outside of that box and seeing where you can bring something new into your business that will create the foundation of recurring revenues and secure the future of your business.

Traditional accounting firms use time sheets and bill for their time at the end of the project. At Sedulo, we don't operate on time sheets, we pre-agree fees for work, and then we do the work regardless of the time it takes.

We have built a recurring fee base of monthly accountancy fees, paid on standing order, that provide a guaranteed regular income in the same way the hosting businesses we acquired to rescue Getupdated did.

All our other services have been built around the skeleton of recurring fees. In the early days, our business model was to ensure our costs were never any higher than the monthly standing order fee. Any project work done on top of this was then profit. As our service portfolio has expanded, we are no longer able to do this, but I wish I could, because I felt a lot safer when I operated this model.

I cannot stress enough how important it is to generate recurring cash flow, and that's why I keep on coming back to this point. Recurring cash flow will give you a solid foundation to build on, and it's this that should give you the confidence to keep pushing organic growth.

Create multiple revenue streams

As your business grows, you need to look for additional revenue streams. These new revenue streams must complement your existing core income.

At the inception of Sedulo, we started out with accounting work. Quickly, I recognised that most of our clients needed tax planning, so we introduced that in year two.

When Just Search became a success, and we sold it in 2007, I realised that all the companies that we were to help grow would eventually need to do some kind of transaction. I brought in a corporate finance offering in year three.

Once the client had sold out, they were then sat on buckets of cash and they didn't know what to do with it, so in year four we introduced a wealth management arm to advise them on how to invest it wisely.

Most companies during growth phases need to fund it, and I felt we didn't have enough funding options for our client base, so we created a banking arm in year six.

Finally, in year nine we bolstered our wealth management team by bringing in a designated mortgage advisor as many of our clients were investing in property.

Each time we spotted that there was an offering our client might require throughout their journey, we bolted it on. This approach also secured one of our core values as a business—of being a provider of holistic advice.

Focus on cash

I mentioned earlier how important cash is. As we identified and grew each new organic revenue stream, I made sure that each new addition assisted our cash position. It is normal for an accountancy firm to have clients that pay, on average, over 90 days from when the work has been completed and billed. This means a £7m turnover accountancy practice could well have a £2m debtor balance. Sedulo couldn't tolerate this since we wouldn't have the financing to support an ongoing situation of being constantly being owed around £2m by debtors.

We purposely added services such as banking, corporate finance, wealth management and mortgages, because these services don't have a mechanism that relies on the generation of invoices or having to await payment. These services are paid on completion of the transaction and often by the provider, perhaps the bank or insurance company, as opposed to the end client. This makes a huge difference to us. It means that, as a firm, we are owed more like £750k at any one time, rather than the £2m we would have been owed if we had been operating in the traditional way. So we have a business model that is more than 50% more efficient from a cash perspective than our competitors.

Do find these new revenue streams, but make sure you try to find ones that generate cash and don't put further pressure on your cash balances if you can help it.

Remodel your business if you need to

One of my clients and good friends is Sandeep Malhotra. Sandeep and his wife Seema—who features in the television programme *The Housewives of Cheshire*—own a great fashion brand called Forever Unique, which I work closely with.

Forever Unique started life buying in product

and wholesaling to retailers, on a sort of cash and carry business model. It then went global through a network of agents and distributors selling a spring/summer collection and an autumn/winter collection on a forward order basis.

Spring/summer collections tend to be sold to retailers in January, and autumn/winter collections are sold in July, but it takes at least a year to design, produce and sell a collection. So for more than a year, there was virtually no cash into the business as it was focusing on generating product for the following year. Whilst it made complete sense to do this, the cash flow implication of this decision was painful. That said, they achieved it, but the cash became lumpy given the delivery of the collections into the hands of its customers mainly took place during only two months of the year.

A few years ago, in order to secure a more constant cash flow, they did what most retailers have done and decided to generate online sales. To do this, they needed to create a whole new feeder brand with a lower price point to suit the online consumer. They had to completely rebuild their business to deal with the fast turnaround of weekly incoming product and the logistical challenges this presented. They grew their team from around 10 of them to almost 50, overnight.

This was a company that had gathered wool on its back, but they utilised almost all of it for the restructuring of their business for further growth. It took a couple of years and a fair amount of pain, but they have since started to see the fruition of the new structure and have grown almost 100% within two years—something they couldn't have achieved with their previous business model and infrastructure. They have also laid the foundations now for future growth.

I have the utmost respect for both Sandeep and Seema because the easy choice would have been to keep doing what they were doing, which had after all already enabled them to grow a successful business. The painful 2–3 years they chose to endure to secure a stronger future for the business has now set them up for far greater success further down the line.

Take some calculated risks

In the main, progress is about making small tweaks and changes, here and there—changes that translate into minimal, but nevertheless ongoing, incremental improvements to your business.

The aviation industry is a fantastic example of how far you can go with incremental improvements, but these take time. I went to a seminar not long ago, and I am not sure whether what I heard were cast-iron facts, but they told me that if I had boarded a flight in 1914, there was a 25% chance of perishing on the flight.

During 2017, I was told, despite there being over 36 million flights, there were no passenger fatalities that year—an astounding statistic and proof of the effectiveness of small constant improvements. But, I repeat, they take time. Sometimes you have to move onto another level entirely, and to do this, you need to do something out of the ordinary.

I was becoming slightly miffed that by 2015 we were—what I considered—the best advisory firm in Manchester and yet no one knew who we were. I was frustrated that we had done such good things, with Just Search and Getupdated for example, and yet were still so under the radar. I also found myself looking back at the first six years and wondering if the amount of time and effort I had put in—7 days a week and almost 100-hour weeks for year after year—had actually been worth it, to have built what I thought was still a small company.

What had happened with Just Search was still fresh in my mind—how well we had done in the first couple of years and how quickly it had come undone as soon as the water had got choppy. There was no way I was going to make that mistake again. I wanted to be sure that the next time we put our head above the parapet, we were sound from the foundation up, both operationally and financially.

We still had no wool on our backs in terms of financial security, but I felt that we had de-risked as much as we could and it was time to take a new chance. I wanted to level up rather than have such, what seemed like, painful and slow progression.

My landlord, Robin, had always been good to me because when Sedulo version 1.0 had owed his company money, I had stuck to my word and made sure it was paid, as I did with every creditor. It was not unusual for us to chat on the phone from time to time or to grab a coffee together when the chance arose.

On this particular occasion when we met for a coffee, Robin said he wanted to show me a new office he'd bought with a view to me possibly moving in. The office, which was on Deansgate in the centre of Manchester, had two floors and a rooftop area, and enough space for around 75 staff on each floor.

I explained that we still had two years to run on our existing lease, which was for a building that Robin no longer owned, and as he wasn't our landlord any more, we weren't in a position to move. All the same, he persuaded me that it was worth taking a look, so I went to see for myself.

As soon as I entered Robin's new office, I could see a lot of potential. I'd had an idea to create an ecosystem that would bring our client base and partners together, and I was going to need an amazing space to do it. It would look a little like a hotel lobby with meeting rooms and a bar area, so staff, clients and corporate partners could just drop in and work there—like these co-working spaces that are now cropping up in cities all over the UK, except that people would be able to use ours for free. We'd also be able to use the space to hold events, which would increase footfall through the business. I wanted a space like no other advisory firm had ever had—with a rooftop bar! Don't ask me why. I wasn't sure myself. I just let my ideas flow.

Robin loved my ideas so much, he agreed to do the whole fit-out for us—if we signed a 10-year lease. This was the "level up" I had been waiting for!

Take a leap of faith

I agreed to lease two floors and the rooftop for 10 years—with enough space for 150 staff, and at the time, only 23 staff to work there! Whilst that seems like a big commitment to make on a property of that size, at the time, there was no way Robin would have fitted it out at his cost for anything less. I had to take the chance.

It was a risky move, but I didn't feel any sense of nervousness. Something told me, in the pit of my stomach, that it was the right thing to do and would pay off. The first thing I had to do, was try to get out of a settlement with my current landlord because we had just signed a 10-year lease in a new place whilst still having a lease to run on our existing one. He agreed a deal that was more than we could afford, so I went to the bank to get a loan to pay the, now, former landlord off.

To save money, I got Zeri involved to help me redesign the place, which was as typical of an accountancy office as you could get—ceiling tiles, brown wooden desks, blue carpet tiles and stacks of grey metal filing cabinets filled with old dusty files.

Consider your audience

Just as we had signed the lease, we were taking our whole team off to Barcelona for what I remember to be one of the best Christmas parties we'd ever had—and we'd had a few!

While we were there, we stayed at a hotel that had once been an old tobacco factory called the Hotel U232. On our first evening there, we chilled in the bar area, which reminded me of a New York-style bar—quite dark with lots of black and wooden effect. That was it! We would replicate this place in our own office—and that's exactly what we did.

The bar only occupied half of the floor area on the first floor, though, so now we had to nail down the meeting spaces. My main worry at this point was that, whilst we would be a great choice of advisor for the typical 20-something-year-old technical entrepreneurs who would walk in and see our bar and decide that we were the right accountants for them, we might not appeal to the older generation at first glance—might they feel alienated and think we were too trendy? Don't forget, the older generation were the ones who had the wealth and had already established successful businesses, so not winning them over did give me cause for concern since large fees existed within them.

I respect my elders anyway, right—so I decided to create an environment that blended the old with the new, and this theme would run through this whole refurbishment as it did later too with the Leeds office that I've mentioned earlier in this book. I sourced an old 1940s-style school blackboard and—ironically—placed it in the Steve Jobs suite we had created.

Along the same lines, I sourced an old bookcase from a monastery in Lincolnshire—and turned it into a sweet shop. It took me four hours to individually pick the sweets to go on the shelves—a mixture of Uncle Joe's mint balls, cough candy, butterscotch and sherbet lemons. This time, I envisaged people coming in and taking the sweets away for themselves or their grandchildren, telling them stories of when they had been given them too as a child, and guess what—it happens all the time.

Be Authentic

Here's that word again—"authenticity". We designed the offices as we went along. There was no design agency. We did it ourselves. Zeri and I bought everything for a bargain price on eBay, and everything in our office has a story as to why it belongs there. It's not that I don't agree with bringing in a design agency to fit out an office. It just wasn't right for us. Almost everything you see in our office has its own why.

It's worth echoing here that we bought everything for a bargain price. You could easily walk into our office and mistakenly think we have spent a small fortune, maybe even think we are a little bit flashy, but trust me, the same principle was applied to this project as we'd applied to our very first office fit-out when we had a cloth-covered boardroom table! It was done on a shoestring budget, but you wouldn't think so if you walked in through our front door.

Incidentally, we made sure the floor for the staff was completely open-plan and the work area was light and refreshing. There wasn't an endless amount of money to spend on decorating it, so we put time and care into every purchase.

I have always been the sort of person who spends extravagantly but only in certain areas, unlike those people who don't spend time on anything but will spend a fortune on basics that can be purchased for much less. That's not me—I purchase big on the things that give the greatest impact.

Get amongst the team

I mentioned that our main staff working quarters are open-plan. Having offices for management is not my style either. I believe it puts barriers up between management and the team, and I really don't see many benefits from sitting in an office on your own with the door closed just to create that hierarchy. Furthermore, sitting in a separate office also means you don't get to hear what's going on across the client base, and that reduces the cross-selling opportunities. I don't even have a desk in our offices—I just go in and work from wherever is free.

As I said, the office looked as though we had spent a fortune. We hadn't. When I walked in on the opening day, I knew in my heart we had arrived. I didn't have a clue how this was going to translate into financial gains. I hadn't extensively thought through how much return on investment we needed to produce to justify it being a success either. I just knew people would start taking us more seriously, and that inspired in me the faith that more than enough revenue would follow—and it did. My gut instinct was correct.

Make your money work for you

This risk paid off for us and was an important step we had to take to reach the next level. But while we were risky in one sense, we ensured we were more effective and efficient in another. Here's another tip on spending your money wisely.

When I walk into most professional firms for example, I notice that they have a whole host of staff who are not fee-earning, receptionists being an obvious one. We don't employ receptionists to answer the telephone at Sedulo. We employ front-of-house events personnel. These people provide a huge amount of value to our brand, they create and run events, raise brand awareness, increase foot flow and ultimately generate additional revenue to our business. They do their work from reception, though, so you do get a nice warm welcome when you walk through the doors—it just doesn't cost me anything!

I don't have a personal assistant either. I have nothing against them and I may get one in the future when I think there is enough work where they can add value, but I think they are often recruited by companies in the early stages more for kudos than because of any increase in efficiency or other requirement.

I talk a lot about taking advantage of opportunities in this book, and this risk taking is essential for your growth plans, but I can't overstress the importance of doing this *within an infrastructure* to minimise the chances of getting it wrong. Once you have built these foundations, you will be well prepared for opportunities that present themselves.

Take action...

1. Grow recurring revenue strings

It's stressful enough running a business as it is. Minimise this by creating revenue streams within your business that are all but guaranteed.

Find a way to get people onto subscription, membership, and retainer-type models wherever you can. Try to find a way because it will ease pressure on short-term performance.

2. Create multiple revenue streams

Don't rely on one revenue stream if you can help it. Think outside the box, and try to find revenue streams that have different payment terms or product margins for example.

Overall, try to reduce risk by not relying on one sole income stream wherever possible.

Chapter XV

Seize Opportunities

In the last chapter, we looked at laying down strong foundations throughout your business's infrastructure. Meticulously building such foundations should allow you to take full advantage of opportunities that come your way, the kind that I describe as "level ups".

These opportunities always seem to present themselves, by the way, when you least expect them and when you are not begging for them.

We have all been there, when it feels as though our luck's ran out and we're praying for things to change, and at that point, we also know...it never does. When you pay less attention to whether things are going your way or not in regard to "luck", things start to drop by your way in the form of opportunity.

Make hay while the sun shines

When it comes knocking, be sure to take advantage. Whilst you need to accumulate wool on your back for the downturns, you also need to make hay while the sun shines. Getting the balance right is something we are all constantly evaluating, and is one of the major causes of my anxiety.

We moved into Sedulo's new Manchester head office in 2016, but there was little point in building such an excellent facility for putting on events only to then call it "Sedulo's office", so we gave it a new name and branding. When we found out that the building was originally called Regency House, we decided to rename our new office as 'The Regency Club'.

The Regency offers free breakfast all morning, afternoon tea after lunch, and free beverages all day—to staff, clients and business associates. It's also available for hire for free.

We have held many different kinds of events, including *Dragons' Den*-type sessions, Empowering Women panels, and one of our clients, the Canadian Rugby League's Toronto Wolfpack, even used the facility for their media press launch.

No one else in our industry is doing this in the same way that we are. Incidentally, in 2017, I had the opportunity to invest in a travel agency called Perfect Getaways, which I eventually did. They were based in a very small shop space, in a tiny village on the Wirral called Little Sutton.

I explained that I would invest in them if they did something different. We decided to mirror what we have done with Sedulo, and create a space that's different. As I mentioned earlier, if you hit on a formula that works, use it time and time again.

I couldn't work out why travel agents, in the main, look so boring when they are meant to be a place to go for booking your holiday. There aren't many things in life more exciting for families than booking their family holiday, yet many of their stores look just like the offices of professional service firms.

So we have created a space that is bright, has an indoor beer garden and bar for the adults, and a sweet shop and games consoles for the children.

Since then, we have rolled out five shops, featuring prosecco bars, gin and ale bars, and we have a plan to very quickly do five more and take the total to 10. It could prove to be a very exciting side investment.

Anyway, coming back to Sedulo, as well as business-orientated events, we also host a lot of social events, and during the Euro 2016 football tournament, we showed almost every game. For the England versus Wales game, we had a packed Regency Club, full of people enjoying eight hours of live music, football and refreshments. It was attended by most of the North's finest professionals, but there was one particular guest who came to that event who would go on to play a huge part in the progression of our business.

Leyton Jeffs had come as a guest of our bank manager. Having previously worked for the funders RBS, Aldermore and Boost Capital, he was about to set up his own debt funding brokerage and approached me after the game for a chat. He explained that he was interested in seeing if we could do something together before making a final decision to go it alone. As the conversation developed, I kept an open mind. Then Leyton brought out his business plan.

He was projecting an estimated turnover of around £400k in his first year, which would be generated from finding businesses funding in the form of mortgages, invoice discounting, factoring, bridging loans, and unsecured loans.

I told him that I didn't think he would hit those targets on his own, but what I did like about the business was that the income would be paid from the funder—not the client—so it would mean we had another service for which we had a positive cash model. This would be strengthening our holistic offering and our cash business model, and it was very scalable.

To be totally honest about it, I felt very fifty-fifty on whether or not to go with it, but I decided to take the chance—apart from a few months of Leyton's salary, there was little risk.

We agreed a 65:35 joint venture in Sedulo's favour, and we set up Sedulo Funding Solutions (SFS).

Leyton absolutely annihilated his business plan. Within the first 12 months, it made EBITDA of £400k. Leyton converted his shares in SFS to shares in the group. Within the first 24 months of SFS, we completed over 400 deals and generated income of over £1.2m.

SFS significantly improved the financial stability of the group as a whole and allowed us to take bigger risks later on. We had been given an opportunity and we had taken it—the England versus Wales event has so far generated well over £1m of revenue for us. This event alone more than justified the move into our new premises.

It's important to note that we don't do things for the sake of it—we try to sweat our assets. When we have a social event, although there is a huge amount of fun to be had, we are focused on getting business from it.

Recently, in partnership with two of our clients, the ticketing business Skiddle and video creative agency Tunafish Media, we held a surprise all-day festival at our offices. None of my staff knew about it, and they turned in for a normal day at the office to find that it had been given a 24-hour make over and had been turned into three floors of festival space, including sniffer dogs, portable toilets and a live performance from UK rap artist Big Narstie.

Whilst it was a crazy event, which went viral and got us some media coverage, we invited clients and potential clients over in the afternoon and signed almost £100,000 worth of clients on the day. This is what our front-of-house team is busy doing, whilst everyone else is hiring receptionists to open doors and answer telephones.

If it's still shining, make some more

As I said earlier, the more you sit around waiting for these breaks, the less chance there is that one will come along. Don't measure your luck and wait for yours to turn up. Get on with doing stuff.

I was busy working on our impending acquisition late 2017 when the next opportunity came my way. Cathryn Wright was a friend who I had known ever since my time at the debt management company where

I had turned around the post room. She had worked in another department for the same company. We had kept in touch loosely as Cathryn lived in London, and as fortune would have it, she now fancied opening up a London office for us—as I mentioned earlier, she had previously been the chief executive of a highly regarded charity for the lesbian, gay, bisexual and transgendered (LGBT) community called Stonewall.

We had no intention of opening in London until Cathryn came up with the idea and suggested that she head it up. Not only do I love Cathryn's approach to work, but as I mentioned earlier, she can also bring some diversity to our boardroom.

Thanks to Cathryn's initiative, we have set up in the capital, and now we intend to build this office up. We signed 100 clients in year one without even having a permanent base. I didn't want us to take a big risk here, which is why we chose to do it organically. Once we have hit a certain size, we will look to expand with an acquisition here, possibly in 2019.

In the next chapter, you will find out that we did a relatively large acquisition, it was large for us, in 2018. Please note that we focused on some organic growth plans to minimise risk and to try to maintain a healthy mix within our overall growth strategy.

And if it keeps shining, make even more!

I am constantly monitoring risk, and for so long as I don't feel exposed to too much potential downturn, I am happy to consider more opportunities, especially when they keep presenting themselves. As I said earlier, though, this all comes with its stresses, and I sometimes wonder why I can't just bloody settle on what I have built already. But I can't.

Another opportunity that came our way in 2018, which was almost impossible to refuse, was the chance to deepen our connection with the sports industry.

We have always looked after football and rugby Super League clubs, and we act for a number of sporting governing bodies, including Basketball England and England Boxing for example.

Our work within the sporting industry has also always included looking after a number of individual sports stars—mainly from the worlds of football, boxing and rugby.

However, in 2018, we had the chance to enter into another partnership in regard to our wealth management division, when we were approached by independent consultant Iwan Roberts. Iwan was already acting for a number of high-profile sports stars, mainly from football's Premier League and Championship competitions.

As someone who is self-made, I hate to see people do well for themselves and then have little to show for it in the end. This happens far too often in the world of sport in particular. I love the fact that we can make a significant difference to these people, although sometimes we have to be quite brutal in our assessment of their financial affairs to get the message across.

We provide a number of services to players, and one of these involves finding commercial properties for them—properties with first-class anchor tenants who are willing to sign 15–25-year leases. By purchasing a number of these over their career, the players can generate a large recurring revenue (there it is again!) that will keep paying them long after they retire from sport.

The partnership with Iwan was another opportunity that presented itself to me that I felt was interesting and low-risk. We had almost £10m of funds under management from these clients alone within the first six months of creating this business unit. It also lead us to our next opportunity.

We were getting mortgages, through our team of IFA's, for our clients to purchase the properties, and we were doing more of them. What we didn't have was a specialist mortgage advisor. Would you believe it? I was contacted by a mortgage broker, a chap called Peter Clarkson, who wanted us to set up a mortgage business with him. It would only take a low level of capital to go ahead with the idea, so we did it. Sedulo Mortgages was set up at the end of 2018.

You know what they say about buses—they all seem to come at once. I have found it to be just as true in business as it is in life. Throughout the early years, I had prayed and begged for a bus to come past, and I had worked 100 hours some weeks, so I felt like I deserved it. But it never came. I had to wait until we had battled for six years, and broken through that £1m revenue barrier first. As I shared with you previously, we hit the £2m mark pretty quickly after that, within one year to be precise, and then the buses came thick and fast.

If you're in that situation now, where you feel like you need a breakthrough, I feel your pain. The only advice I have for you is that you must keep pushing through those barriers—because they do eventually come if you don't quit!

Keep on progressing

There will come a time when the economy turns down, and I will go back to reining in our growth plans and focusing on consolidation. But the time to grow is when the economy is in the boom part of its cycle, as it was in 2018. Despite the current uncertainty in the world with things such as the Brexit issue we have in the UK, I generally still see buoyancy and positivity in the business world. So long as that remains the case, I will focus on structured growth.

In 2019, we are investigating another potential acquisition in Leeds, having been approached directly. On the surface, another acquisition in Leeds makes sense because I would be able to bolt that on to our existing Leeds office, taking costs out and making that business more profitable immediately.

I am also planning for a small acquisition in London, now that we have built a foundation there, and then a larger acquisition in Liverpool. Then we will maybe take a look overseas, to places where our clients are expanding—places like LA and Toronto to cover North America, and Stockholm and Berlin to cover central Europe.

Whether we will get there, I don't know, but I am a strong believer in having big dreams and pushing myself to see where my limits are.

Build a centralised function

In order to take advantage of opportunities that may cross your path, you need to build upon a solid infrastructure. Once we got to around 40 staff, during 2017, I made a decision to bring in a centralised function in preparation for getting to 100 members and beyond. A marketing function had already been brought in way before then to drive growth, so I spent that year building a human resource function, followed by finance and then internal IT.

Again, doing all this reduced profitability somewhat, but I felt that we needed to build this central pillar in preparation for taking a much bigger risk. With this in place, I was able to appoint a managing director—Cathryn. She needed someone to work with her, and as I mentioned earlier, she then brought in her lieutenant, Max, as finance director.

Before I had taken this step, by the way, I had no idea what the difference was between a CEO and an MD. I used to think a CEO had to be someone on a listed board with thousands of staff, but as we grew, I realised that the day-to-day running of Sedulo could be done so much better by someone else—an MD. I was (and am) much better at looking at a vision and pushing us closer towards that, so my time wasn't best spent dealing with staff issues and day-to-day running.

Since I made the decision to appoint an MD, the progress of Sedulo has been expedited because I am able to concentrate "on the business", a phrase you will have heard often.

I urge you to assess where your skill sets are best

placed and to monitor where your time is spent. If there are other tasks that you could be doing which would bring more benefit than the things you are doing, get someone else in to take over your current workload so you can get onto the tasks that will drive the most value. There is a very good argument here for appointing a personal assistant, and I may get one when I feel that the time is right, though it won't be for vanity purposes.

Embrace "the fear"

I have talked about how I am constantly juggling growth with creating infrastructure and taking advantage of opportunity and minimising risks. It is complicated, and it is fraught with fear.

Most of you will understand this feeling of living in constant fear. When you're starting out, you think that this fear is temporary and that as your business grows and becomes more successful, it will leave you. *Wrong!* As you grow organically and create something more successful, you will begin to realise that fear never leaves you.

That stomach churning, frightening and vulnerable feeling—the fear of losing it all—stays with you, and in my case it actually gets worse. I come across very few clients who don't have it, but I have also started to realise that this isn't the problem I once thought it was. In fact, this fear of failing is actually my main motivation and driver, it's what gets me out of bed in the morning and straight on my emails to try to make stuff happen.

I have changed my mindset on the fear of failing,

and I now see it as a necessary tool to get me where I want to get to. So if you recognise that you have these same feelings, as I suspect you might, don't worry about it—you now know everyone has them. You have to learn to live with it, and better than that, if you can learn to embrace it, it can be a powerful tool.

It makes sense when you think about it that the fear gets worse as you get bigger or appear more successful. As we have got larger, and the costs have increased, this anxiety has become worse for me rather than better. When wages were £10k per month, if we didn't get paid, I could find it somehow.

Equally, the impact you have on your business becomes diluted the bigger you are. You no longer have the ability to either find that money personally or perform an action which would allow you to generate it. In the days when I was £10k short for wages, I would sell like crazy to take on a piece of work that would generate that cash. I couldn't possibly do that to pay our wages nowadays. Today, just as you probably do, I have to rely on, and trust, the people in the team to do their part in making sure we achieve what we need to, and this loss of control over the situation takes some getting used to. The dilution of your ability to control the situation is pretty scary, but it's also inevitable.

Get comfortable with your level of financial stability

How much risk you're willing to take, or what opportunities you are willing to explore, is unique to you.

There is no magic formula I can share with you. Across my client base, each have their own metrics that give them comfort, and they are pretty diverse.

You need to identify what financial stability means to you—because it's different for every single one of us.

Let me tell you what it means to me.

Financial stability is the amount of cash I would need to see—either in the bank today or in the immediate future—for me to be able to sleep peacefully at night!

It's as simple as that.

Some of our clients need one year's worth of running costs in the bank to feel financially stable—so if they made no sales for a year, they could still survive. Personally, I am content if we are running with 1–2 months of running costs in our account because I am expecting to earn revenue beyond our costs every month. The recurring nature of many of our income streams gives me a degree of comfort over the future.

If I owned a business that was feast and famine, project-based for example, I would require maybe 5–6 months to feel comfortable. This would mean having to have a lot of capital tied up just to allow me to sleep at night—possibly denying me the opportunity to take advantage of those other chances that can arise.

The amount of financial buffer you require for you to be comfortable is unique to you. You need to find what yours is, but if the size of your buffer is in excess of what you need, perhaps you should be asking how you could be making better use of that cash.

Take action...

1. Get comfortable with your level of financial stability

In order to get yourself in a position where you are happy to take on risk or opportunity, you must first establish a financial position where you can sleep at night.

This is unique to you. Establish where you would feel comfortable and get there as soon as possible.

2. Take advantage of opportunities

Once you have achieved your level of financial comfort, use everything beyond this to take calculated risks to progress your business to the next level. Any cash you have beyond this stability level, if left sat in the bank, is earning you almost nothing today.

Chapter XVI

Identify Game Changers

I talk a lot about levels in this book. That's because I am a big believer that many business owners are so trapped in the day-to-day activities of running their business that they are unable to escape from the level they are at. They can achieve constant incremental improvements, but without spending the time to analyse the situation properly, they fail to identify the huge jumps they can make to reach much greater levels.

Break through that glass ceiling

I work a lot with online e-commerce brands, and I am always staggered at why people concentrate so much on breaking the UK market. It is a great market, without doubt, but it is also highly competitive and the cost per acquisition of new customers can be expensive. To succeed in this type of market, your marketing strategy needs to be highly sophisticated, yet people seem hell-bent on ploughing funds and energy here rather than other markets elsewhere. There are territories that are much larger than the UK and far less mature and therefore less competitive, that may give you a quicker return and faster uplift for your business.

It was during 2017, when Sedulo had reached the point where it was employing around 50 staff, that I decided we needed a large injection to get us to the next level as opposed to continuing with the slow, steady progress we had been making. Given the diversifying we had been doing, I felt we had the ability to take a bigger gamble to get us to where we needed to be quicker, and the sooner the better because I thought we were too small in the market place.

My reasoning for wanting to take a chance on doing something big was driven by what I saw around me. There was a whole pool of competitors of similar size to us in terms of staff and revenue, and most of these were much older than us. Above us in terms of size, of course, were the large accounting firms typically employing hundreds of staff, but there were very few competing in the pool just beneath them—firms which typically employed over 100 staff.

It seemed as though there was some kind of glass ceiling preventing firms like mine from growing beyond the 40–60 staff mark, and I didn't want to remain stuck in this pool. I didn't want to go through the painful process of waiting 3–4 years before taking that next step forward to compete with the firms having 100-plus advisors. It was time to take myself out of the day-to-day mindset and see if an acquisition might be possible.

Buying a company is no different to me than the process of buying any other general life purchase such as a new car or booking a holiday. If you're like me, you are never totally sure you are going to go through with it during the process, and it feels a bit surreal when you have actually done it and find yourself in receipt of your new car or are on your holiday. When I started thinking about buying a business in a different city, I wasn't quite sure I was *actually* going to go through with it.

Test the water first

I was worried whether it was the right thing to do, for a start. I had never done it before, and although we had bought businesses for many of our clients, it's different when it's your own of course. I decided to try a small acquisition first to see how that went. That would allow me to learn some lessons without too much risk. I highly recommend that you do the same. Dip your toe in the water first.

We did just that, and I'm glad we did. In our case, we made a complete botch job of our first acquisition, but it was of such a size that it had little impact other than teaching us the ill of our ways. We started with the acquisition of a very small business, based just outside of Manchester, to test our ability to cope with the acquisition process itself and subsequent integration. We failed miserably!

The vendor (seller) was a lovely, ageing bloke, who was in poor health, and was worried about his long-term ability to look after his clients. He had a client base worth just over £100k, which he was looking after himself. We agreed a deal to purchase it with a small upfront payment followed up with monthly instalments to limit our risk, as the clients were so attached to him. We also retained him for monthly services.

Purchasing in this way proved invaluable because even though the chap sold them to us, he was so attached to them—they were his lifetime's work so that was understandable—that to him they were still *his* client base. So much so, that after we'd sent the letters out engaging them as our clients, he promptly spoke to each of them and said that if there was any problem with us, he would still look after them outside of our agreement.

You can imagine what happened next. Nearly every client decided that the trip into Manchester from Bury was too far, that parking near our city centre office was too difficult, and they didn't want to work with a "big firm", so they would all prefer to stay with him.

We tried in vain to make it work for about three or four months, working on all his clients to convince them we were their best way forward, before deciding to cut our losses—we handed every client back to him and cancelled the agreement on the basis that he had broken it by effectively allowing them to remain with him after we'd bought them. We never fell out with him, though. I completely understand his position, and I wish him all the very best.

We learnt a lot of lessons from this small transaction, which I will share with you:

- You have to win the full buy-in of the vendor for a transaction to work
- Make sure the acquisition is of sufficient size that the vendor is not completely pivotal
- Ensure that there is at least some alignment with processes and systems—in this case, the vendor was still working with paper-based methods, and we couldn't convince his clients that technology has its place
- Even on a small transaction, you need a dedicated "acquisition team" that is focused on the deal

If at first you don't succeed...try again

Our first attempt had been unsuccessful for the reasons outlined above, so the logic was to go for a city centre Manchester practice next, one which was big enough to be employing a few staff and therefore not so reliant on the owner. The target had five staff and a client base worth around £300k, and they worked on similar software to us. We had learnt a lesson or two!

We went through the negotiation process, and the longer the process continued, the more things were bending favourably to the seller's position. Whilst I thought we had agreed everything, he backed out at the last minute. He did us a favour because I was guilty of something I see often in transactions—I had become so emotionally attached to doing the deal that the purchase price had changed considerably, and we were now paying over the odds for the business. He still pulled out anyway, so we clearly didn't have the buy-in of the vendor even at that price. I am thankful that he did the right thing and saved us both a lot of bother.

And again!

We were two attempts in, and I began to wonder if it may end up being a case of third time lucky. *Let's do a much bigger acquisition,* I thought to myself, *and find a firm with more staff and in a different city altogether.* At this point, I am not sure I truly believed, deep down, that we were capable of an acquisition in another city, but I told everyone that was what we were doing, and I decided that it would be Leeds.

Did I research Leeds? Not really. Did I pull together a written business plan? You already know the answer to that question! No.

I didn't purposely go out and look at the competition.

I didn't review the market.

I chose Leeds because that city felt right for us. Simple as that.

Zeri is from Leeds, so I know the city, and I felt that there was a buzz in the place. When we had gone out there, a few years earlier, the nightlife seemed to be behind what I was used to. The restaurants were a bit dated, and the bars didn't have the corporate feel that the ones in Manchester had at that time.

During the previous 10 years in Manchester, a restaurant and bar scene had grown, starting in Spinningfields, the business district of the city, and this had helped transform the city centre as a place to live and work.

I began to notice these establishments opening

in Leeds along with their own independent offerings, and I saw huge development in that city. There was a great feeling of progression about the place, and a really positive atmosphere was being created. Leeds it was!

Visualise your outcome

We were going to need a base in the city. It didn't take us long to find a beautiful building called St Paul's House on Park Square, right in the centre of the city's legal district. This stunning building, built in 1878, faces a park in the middle of the square. Remarkably, the ground floor was free, albeit out of our price range. I spent many a summer day sat on a bench of the park just looking into that amazing space and wondering how on earth I could get us in there—my heart was set on it.

I have never read *The Secret* by Rhonda Byrne, but I have been told that I am a living example of how the "law of attraction", described in the book, works. I can only say that way before there was any chance of us being in that building, I could genuinely see us in there!

I think visualisation is a very important tool, and I often form a picture in my head of the outcome of what I expect my business, indeed aspects of life in general, to look like, and I work backwards from the desired end result to determine the route to make it happen. Almost 20 years ago, for example, I pictured my wedding day, and it played out exactly as I saw it all that time ago. The same has happened constantly throughout my business life, so I encourage my clients to use the power of visualisation as well, and I urge you to do the same. Many of my podcast guests talk of seeing very clearly what their business or family home looked like way before they got there.

Make it happen

Whilst I had been office-hunting, I'd asked our corporate finance team to send out letters to any Leeds-based accountants that had between 10 and 30 staff, to see if there was any appetite to sell. We received a few replies, three of which are worth noting. One of these presented a very similar scenario to our first Manchester acquisition so we steered clear of him. The other two showed more potential.

Out of the two remaining possibilities, one was the perfect size at about 10 staff and £500k revenue. We met with him but I got the feeling, there and then, that the seller wasn't quite ready to give up his client base—we had been there before and it wouldn't have worked.

The third one was too big for us, with turnover in excess of £2m and 35 staff, but we decided to meet them anyway as it's always worth a coffee.

Meeting for the second time, I felt exactly as I had when I had visited the office space in St Paul's House for the second time. *If only we could do something,* I thought. I decided to do the maths.

I knew they should get a consideration of at least equivalent to their annual turnover, and that's what they would expect.

Now I had to figure out a way to get them what they needed without it adversely impacting on the Manchester practice in terms of cash. When it comes to acquisitions, it's always about the cash, so again, whilst I didn't do a written business plan, we spent a lot of time working through various cash flow models.

I found a way to make this acquisition happen without compromising our financial position. I started to get excited, and as we were a business without any notable bank funding at the time, I managed to get the bank on board as well. With a decent amount upfront for the vendors, I was able to put a two-year earn-out in place and offer them an uplift on any additional income we would drive in over those two years.

Don't be greedy

I sent the offer without any great hope of an acceptance because not wanting to compromise the group's position too much, I knew the vendor could get a slightly better offer elsewhere, but to my nervousness and delight, their response was that with a couple of tweaks here and there, a deal could be agreed.

I think this deal went through because it was fair. I am a massive advocate of making sure deals offer equal benefit to both sides, and this one did just that. Too many times, I have witnessed deals where one side wants to haggle with the other to get a better part of the deal. This is where deals usually start to fall apart. I don't get it—the best deals are made quite naturally when both parties feel there's been a fair exchange. So I advise you to try not to be greedy when negotiating transactions of this nature.

We completed the acquisition of Bartfields Chartered Accountants, a company formed in 1927, and coterminously signed a 10-year lease on St Paul's

House on 31st January 2018. On completion of that transaction, Sedulo whizzed from outside the UK's top 100 accountancy firms to somewhere around the top 70. Given that there are around 7,000 such firms, that places Sedulo within the top 1% in the country.

As I mentioned in a previous chapter, almost one year after the acquisition, we have lost very few of the staff we inherited and even fewer of the clients we purchased. We have managed to upsell, on average, 20% more fees from offering our portfolio of services across their clients, and so far the acquisition is proving successful although it is still early days.

We haven't had a cross word with the vendors, and it is likely they will stay with us well past their two year earn-outs, which benefits everyone. Such is the success of the way this transaction has been handled, that we have had other approaches for us to buy other accounting firms, and we will investigate these further. Another acquisition could see us reaching circa 60 staff in Leeds alone, making us a major professional services firm in that city, and that excites me!

Keep searching for game changers

It would have been a long hard road to achieve that same result organically, and that's why I am a big believer in mixing long-term sustainable organic growth with a boost every so often.

I have opted for a boost almost annually with Sedulo in the past few years, and I have a constant eye on them for the future. This constant mix of incremental progression and game changers is what is responsible for the size of our growth. I urge you to look at your business and identify one or two of these yourself.

As for Sedulo, we have a three-year plan, which I mentioned earlier, that places emphasis on us going from £7m revenue as we stand to £14m within the next three years. Within that growth plan are three acquisitions, two of which are within cities where we already have a base and the other is in a totally new city for us.

Almost half of the growth we are aiming for is expected to come from the above "level ups", and we also have an organic growth strategy to hopefully achieve the remaining 50%. This feels like the right mix.

By the time this three-year business plan has been executed, Sedulo will hopefully be a 13-year-old firm with £14m of revenue. It will have taken six years to hit the first £1m milestone and then just another seven years to grow by another £13m.

It has been some journey, and yet, to me it feels like it's only just the beginning.

Take action...

1. Search for game changers and go for them

Don't limit yourself by what you think is achievable. To get real growth, you are going to have to go after something beyond organic growth.

You are going to have to find significant "step ups". Identify one or two of them a year, if you can, and go for them. Mitigate your risk by organic growth and by maintaining your suitable level of financial stability.

2. If you fail at your first attempt, try again

These are high-risk, high-rewards strategies, so you are not going to get them right first time or all the time.

Don't let that deflate or demotivate you. Identify new ones, learn your lesson from the last time, and go for it again.

Epilogue

Who is Paul Cheetham-Karcz?

If nothing else, at least you now know who I am. I am a pretty normal lad from a working-class area, who as a kid, had no idea what his destiny looked like. I just knew I wanted to see what I could achieve. I still don't know where it will all lead, but it is already much better than the system at the time would have had me believe.

I have managed, with the help of copious amounts of people who I am very great for, to be able to achieve a relative amount of success in business and in life. I don't intend to stop here though, and I am busy planning the next stage of progression from a personal awareness aspect as well as a business perspective.

Why I wrote this book

I toyed with writing this book, and then subsequently

dropped the idea time and time again. I didn't want to come across as though I think I am this or that, like a big "I am". That's not why I eventually decided to go ahead with the book and ultimately release it. If anything, it nearly didn't happen for that very reason that I may have come across as being full of myself.

I have explained how new to this success game I am, and I accept that according to some people's definition of success, I am not even there yet. I wouldn't argue with this statement either, and it still does make me cringe to consider myself as a success story. I do recognise I have achieved some things, and if this inspires people who have come from where I have come from to aspire or search to reach their own level of potential, then I will have achieved something by completing this project.
I am still searching to find where my potential lies, hoping that there is still plenty of space between where I am today and where that imaginary glass ceiling above my head exists. I know that this search is going to take courage from me, to keep fighting through the mental pressure that comes with going on this journey.

Having written the book, I am adamant that this was the right time to write my account because the rawness of the content will perhaps resonate with you at some stage, and I hope it helps you to either overcome a hurdle or allow you to avoid one completely.

As I said at the beginning, if you can find one or two things I have shared with you that promote change within your business or life right now, then this book has accomplished its goal. If you return to it further along your own journey, and it provides another couple of answers to your problems, that would be even better!

As a regular user of social platforms, it is my opinion that the aspiring entrepreneur should take a lot of the content that's out there with a pinch of salt. As I have mentioned, it is very rare that the superficial depiction of someone's journey truly mirrors the reality. Hopefully, this book realigns your expectation of what it is really like to live the journey of a business owner.

If you are battling with mental health, I hope this book has given you the reality check that you are indeed not alone. Whatever trials and tribulations you are going through, they are perfectly normal and shared by many, you are not going crazy, and there are changes you can make that will help you to suppress those feelings. Understanding the mental pressures of running your own company are commonplace should give you an opportunity to view them with a different mindset and make them less destructive.

For all of you who are living in the struggle of building your business, I hope my story gives you confidence to carry on through the journey—to keep trying things, to carry on making mistakes and to continue pushing forward—because it would have been a huge mistake for me to have succumbed to my own self-doubts during my journey with Sedulo.

I hope the examples of success that I have referred to in this book, either from my own experiences or those of my clients, provide you with some nuggets of technical advice that you can apply to your own organisation to enable it to prosper. I have gone into great detail on things such as creating infrastructure, and creating a winning team and a culture, because I believe they are the bedrock to any successful business.

I have tried to be as honest as I could, and I have included mistakes where I felt that you might benefit by not making that same mistake as me. I try not to be fearful of failure because that kind of fear is a huge inhibitor to success and progress, and I wish we weren't so scared as a society to fail.

In the introduction to this book, I stated that you wouldn't know who I am or why you should read my book!

Hopefully, I have now answered both of these questions and you judge that reading this book was time well spent.

Thank you for reading and best of luck on your journey.

A tick box to success ☑

Creating a successful business

- ☐ Have a business plan
- ☐ Identify business objectives
- ☐ Make objectives measurable
- ☐ Focus on cash
- ☐ Make decisions with complete clarity
- ☐ Grow from solid foundations
- ☐ Create multiple revenue streams
- ☐ Create recurring revenues
- ☐ Take calculated risks
- ☐ Make your money work for you
- ☐ Make hay whilst the sun shines
- ☐ Put some wool on your back

A tick box to success ☑

Creating a successful team

- ☐ Instil discipline throughout your team
- ☐ Make people accountable
- ☐ Recognise and reward people
- ☐ Educate and develop your members
- ☐ Establish a give and take relationship
- ☐ Embrace diversity
- ☐ Create an external support team
- ☐ Be authentic
- ☐ Define your values
- ☐ Show them what's in it for them

A tick box to success ☑

Creating a more successful version of you

- ☐ Don't let fear hold you back
- ☐ Listen to your gut instinct
- ☐ Believe in yourself
- ☐ Dare to be different
- ☐ Take decisive action
- ☐ If at first you don't succeed... try again
- ☐ Know your why
- ☐ Don't invest for the sake of your ego
- ☐ Step out of your comfort zone

A tick box to success ☑

Creating a healthier version of you

- ☐ Let go of your thoughts
- ☐ Rest
- ☐ Stay hydrated
- ☐ Make sure you exercise
- ☐ Eat well
- ☐ Meditate
- ☐ Have fun along the way

About the Author

Paul Cheetham-Karcz has just turned 40 years old and hails from Reddish, a working-class suburb in Stockport, Greater Manchester. He was educated at a local state school, where he was advised to become a mechanic and sent to a local garage for work experience. On his first day at the garage, even before lunch time, Paul had already decided that he was going to live his life differently.

In his own words, you won't know who he is or the business he runs, which is why he believes now is the time to share his story—before the battle scars of building a business have healed.

Paul is the managing partner of a business consultancy which employs over 100 people in Manchester, Leeds, and London, and his client base includes celebrities from the worlds of sport and entertainment. It's not been an easy ride, and as a result, he has had to learn how to deal with high levels of anxiety, amongst other mental issues, on an almost daily basis.

When he is not closing deals, exploring new business opportunities or ensuring his firm and his clients are on track for future growth and success, Paul enjoys boxing, travel, and meditating—something he recommends for everyone.

Paul is married to his soulmate, actress and business owner Zeriozha, and between them they have three sons.

Acknowledgements

When I started writing this book, I didn't have a clue what I was doing. I just set off typing to see where it ended up, and I'm not even sure I believed, at the time, that it would end up as a book.

I would like to thank the friends and clients I have worked with, who have all contributed greatly to events in my life, particularly those who have allowed me to document, within this book, the parts they played along the way.

To the amazing team at Sedulo, past and present, who strive to make it a better place to work, and who show a consistent desire to do what the client needs to make their business all the better for it. A special thank you to Adam White, Neil McAdam, Lizzy Doherty and Alicia Ambrose-Bayly, who have helped with both the podcast launch, and the release of this book.

To Martin Morrison, who has not only been a great editor, but has also encouraged me and shown at least as much enthusiasm as me to get this book finished. There were times when I thought this book was crap, and he gave me the confidence to continue the journey.

To Teddie Dahlin of New Haven Publishing, who was instrumental in getting this book to completion, and who has taken a chance on me as an unknown writer.

Finally, thanks to all the people who have supported me over the nine months it's taken me to finish the book, allowing me to take more of a back seat away from the office and the house while I focused on getting it over the line.

Lightning Source UK Ltd.
Milton Keynes UK
UKHW040757240420
362180UK00001B/44

9 781912 587193